PROCLAMATION:
Aids for Interpreting the
Lessons of the Church Year

SERIES C

Gerard S. Sloyan
and
Howard Clark Kee

FORTRESS PRESS   Philadelphia, Pennsylvania

COPYRIGHT © 1974 BY FORTRESS PRESS

Library of Congress Catalog Card Number 73–88347

ISBN 0–8006–4058–6

4061A74   Printed in U.S.A.   1–4058

General Preface

Proclamation: Aids for Interpreting the Lessons of the Church Year is a series of twenty-five books designed to help clergymen carry out their preaching ministry. It offers exegetical interpretations of the lessons for each Sunday and many of the festivals of the church year, plus homiletical ideas and insights.

The basic thrust of the series is ecumenical. In recent years the Episcopal church, the Roman Catholic church, the United Church of Christ, and the Lutheran and Presbyterian churches have adopted lectionaries that are based on a common three-year system of lessons for the Sundays and festivals of the church year. *Proclamation* grows out of this development, and authors have been chosen from all of these traditions. Some of the contributors are parish pastors; others are teachers, both of biblical interpretation and of homiletics. Ecumenical interchange has been encouraged by putting two persons from different traditions to work on a single volume, one with the primary responsibility for exegesis and the other for homiletical interpretation.

Despite the high percentage of agreement between the traditions, both in the festivals that are celebrated and the lessons that are appointed to be read on a given day, there are still areas of divergence. Frequently the authors of individual volumes have tried to take into account the various textual traditions, but in some cases this has proved to be impossible; in such cases we have felt constrained to limit the material to the Lutheran readings.

The preacher who is looking for "canned sermons" in these books will be disappointed. These books are one step removed from the pulpit: they explain what the lessons are saying and suggest ways of relating this biblical message to the contemporary situation. As such they are springboards for creative thought as well as for faithful proclamation of the word.

This volume of *Proclamation* has been prepared by Gerard S. Sloyan and Howard Clark Kee. Reverend Professor Sloyan, a priest of the diocese of Trenton, N.J., is chairman of the Department of Religion at Temple University, where he lectures in New Testament. He has published two books of homilies, *To Hear the Word of God* and *Nothing of Yesterday Preaches* (New York: Herder and Herder, 1966 and 1967), was English editor of The New American Bible (1970), and has most recently written *Jesus on Trial* (Philadelphia: Fortress, 1973), a redaction-critical study of the trial narratives in the Gospels. The exegete, Professor Kee, is Rufus Jones Professor of the History of Religion and Chairman of the Department, Bryn Mawr College, Bryn Mawr, Pa. He has taught at the University of Pennsylvania and Drew University, and has been a member of archeological expeditions to Shechem, Pella (Jordan), and Ashdod. His more recent publications include *Jesus in History* (New York: Harcourt Brace Jovanovitch, 1970), *Origins of Christianity: Sources and Documents* (New York: Prentice Hall, 1970), and the third edition of *Understanding the New Testament* (New York: Prentice Hall, 1973), of which he, F. W. Young, and K. Froehlich are joint authors. Professor Kee is a lay member of the United Presbyterian Church.

Introduction

No portion of this book is intended for pulpit use.

The authors have done some writing about the lessons of the last Sundays of the church year. They have done no preaching. Obviously, they could not, since proclamation means entering into the lives of *hearers* so as to engage them in greater commitment to the gospel. Writing on liturgical readings for unknown preachers is necessarily an exercise that is general in character. The man at the typewriter can attend to no local situation, he feels no specific economic threat, he experiences no loss in death or joy in marriage for those in distant pews. Most crippling of all, he cannot know the news of the world or the locality that has marked the preceding week. In brief, "He has nothing to say to my people."

This *caveat* for the *emptor* is not intended to disarm all criticism. The limited task the writers undertook might have been done better, like anything human. But that is not the point of these remarks. The point is that preaching by its very nature is an intensely personal exchange between speaker and hearer. Every homily is a dialogue homily in its inner dynamics. If not, it does not matter what is said since nothing will be heard.

The hermeneutical problem from Sunday to Sunday consists of taking a twofold point of view, that of the ancient inspired writers (insofar as that is possible) and that of the modern preacher, and bringing them somehow together into one. The horizon of the exegete is closer to that of the biblical writers than that, say, of the common reader. It can be adopted in some measure by any perceptive reader whose task it is to preach. The horizon of the homiletical interpreter is so personal and so limited that it probably can be adopted by no one. It may be examined with brief interest but it must be replaced by the horizon of the reader who means to write a sermon. That outlook should somehow be common to the preacher and his hearers on the ancient principle, "Like pastor, like people." Another old saw has it that love either finds or makes two alike. So it is with congregations and their ordained teachers. The weekly business of instruction is, more basically, an attempt to exhort hearers to adopt the preacher's point of view, to do both as he says and as he does. No one can have that standpoint, those ideals, but the preacher himself.

Yet Christian life is not so individual an affair as the above might indicate. There are common attitudes, a common heritage, common obstacles to the everyday living of this life. There is also for the homilist recourse to the thoughts of exegetes and preachers other than himself whose task is likewise the ministry of the word. One can presumably come on an apposite thought in a book of interpretations of the liturgical lessons; it is not only experience combined with daily newspapers and current reading and conversation that sheds some light on life.

The mistake would be to suppose that a book of this sort can supply very much help. At most it can orient the reader toward thinking biblically about the world he and his people inhabit. The writers of the pages that follow try to do just that, to build a bridge between the world of the Bible and the world of everyday. It is not so easily done. The exegete is a historian and literary critic who searches the Scriptures primarily for their faith meaning. The homiletician is a searcher of themes, inner connections among the readings—"Scripture interpreted by Scripture"—yet never in a merely affective way but with a view to the intelligibility of the divine word. Both have something to contribute; either alone or the two together are inadequate as resources. The missing ingredient is the *Sitz im Leben der jetzigen Kirche*, the actual, lived faith community in the midst of which there must be exchange over the meaning of the gospel. Only the individual homilist can supply that out of the experience of his people's and his own life.

The learning of the learned can be oppressive or it can be liberating. The same is true of anecdotes, historical vignettes, real-life examples. A healthy reaction of preacher and hearer is: "To be sure, they happened— to Simon Peter, to Napoleon Bonaparte, to the writer. The trouble is, they didn't happen to me." This principle of resistance is so potent that, in a sense, the better a sermon is, the worse it is. As a vicarious experience it is almost worthless. As an invitation to reflect on one's own experience while enlarging it ever so slightly, it can have merit.

The primary value of a book such as this is the help it affords in knowing what not to preach on. Thus, biblical arguments of doubtful worth and dependable scholarship so recondite that it has no place in the pulpit can both be identified here. The turn of phrase that would never rise to the reader's lips, the insight that is clearly not his own, the learned reference outside his normal interests—all these are to be rejected on sight. Yet all of us learn from what we read. It happens constantly. We tend to take things in a different way from the way they appear on the printed page. That is because our matrix of experience is different. Thus, if we see a word of Jeremiah that speaks to us, a phrase of Jesus that strikes us forcibly, a reminiscence from another's pen—all can become our possessions if we take them in after our fashion. "Whatever is received," the scholastics used to say, "is received in the manner of the recipient." There is wisdom here. What a book can teach is in proportion to what we knew or had lived before we picked it up. This is preeminently true of "aids to interpretation" like the books of this series. The interpretation must be the proclaimer's own by the time it is spoken or it is not worth expressing. Unless he has made it *his* gospel, in St. Paul's sense, there will be no valid proclamation.

No attempt has been made to construct a theology of the last eight Sundays of the church year. They fall in the autumn season and coincide with the High Holy Days of our Jewish brothers and the month of Ramadan in Islam. Congressional and gubernatorial elections, football, and Thanksgiving are realities of this season. They have not been attended to. The essence of "salvation history" is that the autumn 1974 part of it has not yet happened at the present writing.

But all this preacher and people know. They need no printed books to tell them. What they do require is a living voice to give tongue to the thoughts of many.

Gerard S. Sloyan

Temple University and
Our Lady of Mercy Church
Philadelphia, Pennsylvania

Table of Contents

The Twentieth Sunday after Pentecost

Lutheran	Roman Catholic	Episcopal	Presbyterian and UCC
Hab. 1:2–3; 2:2–4	Hab. 1:2–3; 2:2–4	Hab. 1:2–3; 2:2–4	Hab. 1:1–3; 2:1–4
2 Tim. 1:3–14	2 Tim. 1:6–8, 13–14	2 Tim. 1:6–14	2 Tim. 1:3–12
Luke 17:1–10	Luke 17:5–10	Luke 17:5–10	Luke 17:5–10

EXEGESIS

First Lesson: Hab. 1:2–3; 2:2–4. Living at a time of moral corruption within his own nation and of military threat from neighboring nations, the prophet Habakkuk cries out in protest to God. His pleas to Yahweh for help (1:2) have so long gone unanswered that he is challenging God directly: it is no longer a matter of the prophet's petitioning God to deal with the violence and injustice that is everywhere. Now the issue is God's own justification of himself for failure to deal with the moral disorder that characterizes the prophet's own fellow countrymen. The implication of v. 3 is that even if God persists in allowing these wrongs to go unchallenged, it is incomprehensible why he insists on troubling the prophet by requiring him to witness these unrequited misdeeds. The prophet's mood is like that of Job, who complained to God: "I cry to thee and thou dost not answer me. . . . Thou hast turned cruel to me" (Job 30:20–21).

In desperation the prophet sets himself up as a watchman on a tower (2:1) as earlier prophets had done (Isa. 21:6–9; Jer. 6:17; Ezek. 3:17), waiting for God's word or act—the message which he might then transmit to the people. And the message that does come is an affirmation of the fidelity of Israel's God. It is to be posted publicly, in large and legible letters, so that those who read it may hasten to pass the word on. The vindication of God, which is to take place when he acts to set matters right among his people and throughout the creation, will not be long delayed. The "end" when God's purpose will be accomplished is near at hand.

When God thus acts to vindicate his name and to deliver his people from injustice within and oppression from without, mankind will be divided into two groups: those whose lives are perverted and contorted by their foolish attempts to live out of their own resources, and those who

1

live in reliance upon God and his trustworthiness. To say that the former are not "upright" in "soul" (v. 4*a*) is not to imply that some ill-defined inner dimension that we might call "soul" or "spirit" is not dominant over the material aspects of their existence, but is to make the much more sweeping charge that the whole range of their existence is out of harmony with the divine will. As a result, they are "puffed up," according to one reading of the Hebrew text, or they are simply failures, as RSV translates. But those whose lives are ordered according to God's purpose live not on their own shaky resources but out of the limitless reservoir of God's faithfulness ("faith") to his covenant people. This is the reality that offers the answer to the prophet's initial despair.

Second Lesson: 2 Tim. 1:3–14. The counterpart of the faithfulness of God to man affirmed by Habakkuk and appealed to by Paul in Rom. 1:17 is God's having entrusted man with the gospel. Writing in the name of Paul, though at a time when the Christian faith was being handed down through successive generations (v. 5), the author of this letter reminds his readers that faith cannot be passed on like a legacy; rather, each new generation requires a reaffirmation of the faith and a rekindling of the Spirit of God, if faith is to be a reality. But faith cannot exist outside the context of courage, of love, of disciplined life (v. 7), and above all, of suffering. Even so, the responsibilities of faith are not meritorious works that qualify those who accept them to share in the life of the community of faith. All that the faithful receive comes to them as a gift, not as a reward for services rendered (v. 9). The fact that God has already revealed himself in Jesus Christ, and in him has already triumphed over death shows that the victory of faith is God's achievement, not ours.

The guarantee of the fidelity of the Christian to the witness that he is now called and privileged to bear is not an inborn quality of perseverance but the effect of the faithfulness of God to preserve to the end what he has begun and to bring to consummation his purpose through and for his people. Writing at a time when the church had to consolidate its authority and define more precisely what it is that faith affirms, the writer of this letter assumes the name of Paul and draws on the authority of the Pauline tradition. In doing so he expresses confidence that the pattern and substance of sound doctrine will be maintained by the work of the Spirit within the community of faith (v. 14), and that this will continue to be so until the day of consummation (v. 12).

Gospel: Luke 17:1–10. The Gospel lesson focuses attention on the day-to-day implications of the life of faith, which it depicts in a most realistic manner. Whenever any human community exists—even that of the followers of Jesus—some members are bound to constitute problems and stumbling blocks for others. But no one can live obediently within that new covenant community while continuing to think only of himself or to limit consideration of the implications of his decisions and actions to their significance for him as an individual. The life of faith demands avoidance of actions that may harm others, and forgiveness of others whose actions harm us. Willingness to forgive is not to be limited by the commonplace declaration: "I'll forgive you this time, but don't let it happen again." Like the grace of God, the availability of forgiveness is exactly equivalent to human failure: seven times for seven injustices.

But faith must be not only conciliatory: it must be daring, reaching out against human calculation or expectation. So rare a commodity is it (v. 6) that a little goes a long way. Faith that might be considered to be as insignificant or as microscopic as a tiny, common seed can be the instrument of spectacular results, here described in terms of typical Semitic hyperbole.

The lesson closes with a parable, which argues from the lesser to the greater: if a human master can expect selfless performance from his earthly servant, how much more should God's servants be willing to go beyond routine or explicit commands in order to serve him? The pattern of service to God is not based on specific acts in conformity to specific commands. On the basis of what is appropriate for the Master, faithful service goes beyond what is required or expected. To live thus is to be a worthy servant.

HOMILETICAL INTERPRETATION

When we read in the newspapers of murderous shootings and bombings in Northern Ireland, of forcible detentions in the Philippines, of the harassment of populations in Uganda, South Africa, Chile, and the Soviet orbit, we tend to make little connection between those harsh realities and the Bible. We call the Bible a literature of consolation. We use religious-sounding words like "adversity," "faith," and "stronghold." Even the stark vocabulary of warfare, of reprisals against citizens, becomes mere "contention" and "strife" in our verbal laundering process.

The Babylonian (or Chaldean) threat to Israel was about as gentle, in its outworking, as the Stalinist purges of the 1930s. It can be compared to the irrational murders of the IRA or the Ulster Defense Association. When Habakkuk cries out to the Lord, "Violence!" that is exactly what he means. It was only the refinements of warfare that differed from ancient to modern times. As to the effects, they were quite the same: the wiping out of villages, loved ones butchered and left in the dust, and the threat of extinction of nations and of peoples.

The All-Powerful, then as now, seemed powerless.

Sacrifice and psalmody in Israel's temple began to resemble a charade: pomp and circumstance directed to—no one. Subsequently, those High Holy Days during two millennia of persecution in Europe were much the same. So, too, those solemn masses, that turning to Mecca at the muezzin's call, those challenges to personal reform in pulpit preaching, much of it heeded—all for naught, as babies lay sucking at the breasts of dead mothers, as the conqueror's heel dug deep into the lands of those whose boast was in their God.

Habakkuk is not speaking about woes like losing one's job or suffering the loss of aged parents. He writes of a God who does not answer in the midst of a carnage calculated to destroy all trust in him.

Finally, an answer comes back through the prophet: the Lord needs time. Some of his designs make sense after a century or two. Others do not come to light so quickly. Yet the vision will come clear. That it will is sure. There will be no delay—but on God's time schedule, not man's. His haste is not our haste. "If [the vision] seem slow, wait for it" (Hab. 2:3).

Justice will be done in due time. Live out your life as a just one, as a pious Jew, in a spirit of trust. Impatience gets you nowhere, whereas faith in the mysterious designs of the Lord gets you everywhere.

Not long ago, in Washington's Union Station, a little girl was sitting with her mother, chafing at the train's lateness. She just *had* to get where she wanted to go. Her mother could be heard saying to her, philosophically: "Might as well relax, honey. You goin' to be waiting like this all you' life."

Waiting for Amtrak. Waiting for Godot. Waiting for the Holy One of Israel—whose answer sometimes comes in gas chambers and machine gun volleys.

"Increase our faith," the disciples said in their naive hope of perfect justice—scarcely knowing what Habakkuk knew. They got from Jesus an answer like the one that came to the prophet. Mustard seeds ordering sycamine trees around the landscape. Century-old roots upended, sinking beneath the surface of the sea. "If the vision seem slow, wait for it."

The unworthy servant carries out orders . . . and waits. He does no more than his duty. Correcting one another, forgiving, avoiding scandal: the daily round of life. Seven times a day; some days more than that.

Faith, the waiting game. Faith, the truth entrusted. Faith, the rich deposit.

The letters to Timothy have a bad press in theological circles because they represent the third generation of Christianity, at least. The early dynamism is gone, some scholars say. "Faith" is no longer the eschatological decision that it was in Jesus' parables, the key to salvation that it became in Paul's great letters. Faith is "the faith" now, the pious possession of one's grandmother—who is modern enough to be named Lois. At least she was a "young" grandmother. But the gift of God has gone cold, Timothy is told, and needs rekindling. The sound words once delivered are in danger of being departed from.

The writer hints that "Timothy" should be pronounced "timidity," since he does not have sufficient awareness of God's power. There is even the intimation of trust in human works rather than in God's grace. Then the notion of God's "purpose" appears, and we are back at square A: the vision spoken of by Habakkuk; Luke's trees thrown into the sea.

There is a way out of all this and some have taken it. It is the way of verbal assertiveness, usually in loud tones. Preacher, apostle, teacher. What do those words mean, some ask, if not "a bold declarer of the truth"? The promise of persecution is even held out, which for many makes the proposal that much more attractive. To be right in religion and by that fact superior all one's life; then to be humiliated and rejected at the end. Who could ask for anything more?

The biblical writers could, and they do.

They want fidelity to a holy calling—an archaic way of saying "hang on through thick and thin."

They want patient waiting for a vision of God's purpose. Patience can mean fifty-five years.

They want a share of suffering for the gospel, which life itself will bring if the gospel is taken seriously. No pilgrimages to Compostela, no preaching to unbelieving hordes, no doorbell ringing. Living. That should do it. Provided, of course, there is a lively sense of the Christ who abolished death and brought to light life and immortality.

Jesus is so matter-of-fact when he tells a tale about the way the world goes that it is unnerving. Landowners bark orders; slaves shape up. They do it or else. That is Jesus' brusque picture of human dealing which he employs to invite thought of man before God. You can not call it sentimental. There is little room for Walter Mitty dreaming. But doing "no more than our duty" has, upon examination, a certain demanding character about it. It evidently includes avoiding dragging others down to the level of one's own meanness. Straightening others out is another part of duty. Forgiveness is still another.

"I never knew a man," said William Roper, "who was so hard on himself and so easy on everyone else." He was speaking of his father-in-law, which is remarkable enough in itself. Roper had married Meg, the daughter of Sir Thomas More.

Habakkuk and Luke and 2 Timothy all invite us to a life like that.

About the wars we began with, from the Chaldean threat to the latest hand grenade thrown, what about them?

They have something to do with a class which the Bible classifies as "the wicked." Some of the wicked break into homes in Derry or train howitzers on villages in the Middle East, but many of them live in our cities and go to our churches. They make what the guerrillas throw. They do not wish the money to stop so they call everything "defense," just like the governments and the guerrillas.

And the answer of faith to all that? In Habakkuk's time it was, "If the vision seems slow, wait for it." Jesus moved things along somewhat. As between tossing trees and the destroyers of men (millstones around their necks, like hippie pendants) into the sea, he does not seem to have a preference. He is as enthusiastic for the one as for the other. Both are signs of the coming of the reign of God.

Waiting for God while your lands and your family are destroyed before your eyes is a terrifying venture in faith. There are men and women alive in our time who have survived it.

The biblical authors have another string to their bow, a thought or two on "What to do till the destruction comes." It is a word that is not too hard for us, nor is it far off. We need not go up to heaven nor over the sea to bring it, that we may hear it and do it. It is very near us, in our mouth and in our heart.

It is a word that tells us to avoid destroying the souls of others, to strengthen them at need and not drive their weakness to greater weakness still, to speak and act as if Jesus Christ had died for someone and brought immortality to light.

Centuries ago, an unknown Indian wrote, "The Spirit that is in my heart is smaller than a grain of rice, or a grain of barley, or a grain of mustard-seed, or a grain of canary-seed. That is the Spirit that is in my heart, greater than the earth, greater than the sky, greater than heaven itself, greater than all these worlds" (*Chandogya Upanishad* 3, 4).

He, too, knew something about dancing trees.

The Twenty-first Sunday after Pentecost

Lutheran	*Roman Catholic*	*Episcopal*	*Presbyterian and UCC*
Ruth 1:1–19a	2 Kings 4:14–17	Ruth 1:8–19a	2 Kings 5:9–17
2 Tim. 2:8–13	2 Tim. 2:8–13	2 Tim. 2:8–13	2 Tim. 2:8–13
Luke 17:11–19	Luke 17:11–19	Luke 17:11–19	Luke 17:11–19

EXEGESIS

First Lesson: Ruth 1:1–19a. Though the story told in the Book of Ruth is said to have occurred during the period of the Judges (before 1000 B.C.), the language and contents of the work point to the fourth century B.C. as the actual time of writing. Then Judaism was faced with the problem of maintaining the purity of the covenant people even while opening up the covenant blessings to Gentiles, whose interests in Jewish faith were mounting. Ruth is written to deal with that dilemma.

As was the case with the migration of the tribes of Israel to Egypt, in which the seeming catastrophes of the famine in Palestine and the enslavement in Egypt provide the occasion for God's providential deliverance of his people in the exodus, just so the apparent tragedies of the forced migration to the East Jordan country of Moab and of the death of Elimelech's two sons provide the opportunity for tracing the outworking of God's grace to the Gentiles and for discerning how through a faithful Gentile woman he had prepared for the birth of Israel's ideal king, David (Ruth 4:21).

The death of the two sons (1:5) would normally have called into oper-
ation the Israelite law (Deut. 25:5–10) requiring the next of kin to have
intercourse with the widows in order to guarantee that their genealogical
line would not die out. But there were no close relatives in the land of
exile, and no sons of Naomi back in the region of Bethlehem. Nevertheless, Ruth refused to be parted from her mother-in-law or to abandon the
worship of Israel's God (v. 16). By an oath she declared her fidelity to
the family of her late husband and to Yahweh, their God. By returning
to Bethlehem (v. 19*a*) she made possible—without knowing the outcome
—that she would be wedded to a relative of her husband (2:1) and that
the child born to them would be the ancestor of David. Her act of devotion in abandoning home and family is thus rewarded in a manner that
results in blessing for Israel and through her for all the nations.

Second Lesson: 2 Tim. 2:8–13. Service to David's greater Son, Jesus
Christ (v. 8), requires the utmost in discipline, self-sacrifice, and even
suffering. The author speaks of his imprisonment only to contrast his
condition with the wide-ranging, unrestricted power of the gospel which
cannot be bound by fetters nor restricted in its activity (v. 9). The cost of
discipleship he sketches vividly in the lines of an ancient hymn (vv. 11–
13), and he does so in words which depict actual experiences rather than
an abstract or hypothetical pattern of spirituality.

The facets of this life of dedication to Christ are martyrdom (v. 11),
perseverance (v. 12), refusal to recant of the faith (v. 12*a*), fidelity (v. 13).
The author was probably writing in the early second century, building on
the tradition and writing under Paul's name, as Jewish writers had de-
veloped the traditions of Moses, Solomon, Enoch, and others centuries
after the exodus and the age of the patriarchs. Beginning in the time of
the emperor Domitian (A.D. 81–96) and especially in the reign of Trajan
(98–117), Christians were at times required to renounce the faith under
penalty of death. With such a prospect of the trial of faith a present
possibility rather than a merely theoretical idea, Christians had to prepare
themselves in advance. What resources were available to them when they
had to choose between the faith in Christ and life itself?

The answer to this question was clear and unequivocal. Those who
bore testimony to their faith by accepting death at the hands of the
authorities were promised life in the age to come. Those who endured in
spite of hostility and discouragement were to share in the kingdom of

God. Those who refused to stand firm in their testimony would forfeit their share in the final vindication by Christ. Yet even for the wavering, there is the assurance of God's faithfulness to his promise, since what is at stake is not so much the faith of man as the credibility of God.

Gospel: Luke 17:11–19. Not only did Jesus risk ceremonial defilement by passing through the territory of Samaria (v. 11), but he went so far as to extend the benefits of God's grace to a Samaritan in spite of his being a member of that group so despised by Jews. The Samaritans claimed to be the true religious heirs of the tribes of Israel, with their center of worship at Shechem (Joshua 24), and their own edition of the Law of Moses as well as their own historical chronicles. The Jews as descendants of the southern tribes, of which Judah was the most prominent, with their central shrine in Jerusalem, scorned the Samaritan claim concerning shrine, heritage, and Law, and denounced them as half-breeds who had perverted the traditions of Israel.

Commendably reluctant to pollute Jesus by touching him, the ten lepers in the village remained at a distance and cried out for help. Word had obviously reached them of his extraordinary powers, and all of them sought his help in being delivered from this loathsome disease. The term by which they addressed him is a title of respect, *epistata*, without special religious connotations and with no hint of messianic overtones. In light of the variety of cures of leprosy, the command that they should show themselves to the priest was a strange one, even though there was provision for this priestly attestation of the cure of leprosy in the Jewish— and Samaritan—law (Lev. 13:49; 14:1 ff.). In this story the mode of cure is not disclosed and the circumstance of healing is only implied; more important rather are the results; as they obeyed the word of Jesus they were healed (v. 14).

Even so the main point of the story lies not in the fact of healing but in the response of those healed. The gratitude of the despised outsider stands in sharp contrast with the ingratitude of those beneficiaries of grace who considered themselves to be within the community of faith.

HOMILETICAL INTERPRETATION

Old faithful, we rode the range together,
Old faithful, in every kind of weather. . . .

The same West from which that cowboy ballad came celebrates Old Faithful geyser, a marvel of constancy in the regularity of its performance. You can set a watch by its periodic eruption. Fidelis the Roman martyr was the archetype of all the baptized, a class which the North African church termed *fideles*.

Not many years past, there was a mother in Cuba who had a son. In faith she named him Fidel.

The world has done something with fidelity quite other than look to the bond between Christ and the Christian, between man and God. With an almost Pauline instinct it has centered on human love, the foreshadowing of the love between Christ and his church, and identified "fidelity" exclusively in terms of lovers and other strangers.

The poet's constant lover maintained his stance for three whole days together, crediting "that very, very face" as the cause: "Love with me had made no stay,/Had it any been but she."

Cynara's lover was faithful in his fashion but hers was a "bought red mouth." He, for his part, was desolate and sick of an old passion. Shakespeare put it better. Love is that "ever-fixèd mark," he said, which alters not before Time's sickle but bears it out "even to the edge of doom." If it is not faithful it is not love.

The Book of Ruth tells a tale of fidelity which at first seems to be faithfulness to the memory of a dead husband, manifested in love for a mother-in-law. On closer inspection it proves to be a story of the Lord's fidelity to his people, a story which has its beginnings in David's city Bethlehem. There is more to it, however, than that. The brief book polemicizes artfully in favor of mixed marriage at a time when the rigidity of the postexilic reforms of Ezra were in full control.

If the ancient tale knows how to praise a foreigner, the Moabite Ruth, so does Jesus in a later age. It is the Samaritan leper who is found grateful. He remains faithful to the God of his fathers even though the sons of Ephraim and Judah will have nothing to do with him. Jesus' point is that the outsider recognizes the deeds of God despite his double disadvantage as Samaritan and leper.

The author of 2 Timothy has enshrined a saying that he calls "sure" (v. 11) in the sense of "trustworthy" or "dependable." The faithful utterance is about a faithful Christ. Faithless conduct by one lover in face of the anguished fidelity of another is one of literature's oldest themes. We have it here. Though we be faithless, the snatch of hymnody says, he remains faithful. Christ will bear it out—has borne it out—even to the edge of doom.

The patient endurance counseled throughout the NT is worth examining. It is an Israelite heritage, needless to say, hence not identical with the "fate" of the Greeks or any calculated apathy in the philosophical sense. Nowhere do you find Jewish advice to abstain from emotional states or excessive joy and sorrow as you do in Hindu sources. Endurance in the Bible means the active acceptance of suffering at the hands of a mysterious God who need not explain himself. If trial comes, it is either in punishment for sins or else for some corrective purpose that escapes the sufferer. There is no relished self-pity, least of all a spirit of masochism in the Bible. Pain endured for its own sake is thought to be an absurdity.

Pain endured for some purpose known to God, which he has no intention of divulging, is at the heart of biblical faith. However, the matter does not, indeed cannot end there. The only God believed in is one who will vindicate at the end. He will make things right in his good time. This takes us back to some reflections of last week. Faith, in the Bible, is basically trust that God will do what he has said. He is faithful in that active sense. The believer is faithful as a recipient, in his positive assessment of that fidelity.

Volumes have been written on the "faith" of the NT—Paul's outlook in particular—as a Greek departure from a Jewish idea. The Jew saw faith as trust, it is said, total openness to God's uncertain future. The Hellenic world affirmed that its gods had done or would do certain things on behalf of their devotees. The Christian gospel was deeply infected by this Greek spirit, it is further said. Even such proclaimers of faith as that Pharisee of Pharisees Paul were not immune. Hence, "faith in Jesus Christ" was not so much trust in God as acceptance of the proclaimed message that he had died and been raised up for the justification of sinners.

The debate has been acrimonious and could be endless. It is in any case unprofitable, leading to statements like "Hebraic is better" or "Hellenic is better"; "Propositions are bad"; "Faith *in* . . ." is splendid but "Faith *that* . . ." is deplorable.

The church does not need another ideological split like that which tore it apart four centuries ago: faith-driven debates over the nature of faith. No more does it require partisan testimony to Christ which puts Judaism

on one side of a faith wall and Christendom on another. If Christendom
(a social reality) began to be Christianity (a faith reality), it would dis-
mantle the wall from its side, after the example of the one who tore down
the barrier that stood between us.

Faith is fidelity to a lover, in our fashion. The Christian's fashion,
unlike that of Cynara's lover, should be patient endurance.

Jesus said of a sinful woman once that much would be forgiven her
because she loved much. He had a way of discerning love in the most
unlikely types: streetwalkers, foreigners, officers in the army of occupa-
tion. He found it because it was there. His Father did not have any
ethnic or other tests in planting love in human hearts. The God who is
faithful elicits a response of faith where and how he will.

A memoir appeared some twenty years ago describing a boy's growing
up in the last century. It was entitled *A Hostage to Fortune*, part of an
old proverb about marrying a good wife. One of the chapters described
the political situation of the lad's youth as "Paradise Partitioned." That is
a good description of life in the church of Christ—a kingdom divided
against itself. How can the citizens of that realm be characterized? Often
as a people with frontiered hearts.

The widow of Chilion (or was it Mahlon?) in the book that bears her
name saw things otherwise. She did not seem to know about all the
ancient barriers to fidelity. Her ignorance was such that she conceived
the world as a single place. Fidelity to family, to friends, to Godhead
itself was but one reality for Ruth.

An American visiting Yugoslavia recently, well-married and just as well
ordained, found himself a visitor in a convent of Orthodox nuns. He had
been described in an introduction—all parties were speaking German—as
a theologian from the United States. The visit went well. The talk was of
things of the spirit, things of Christ and of the church in that country. He
was dressed, quite by accident, in dark clothing which included a turtle-
neck sweater. At the end of the visit the prioress fell to her knees and
kissed an onyx ring which he had worn for years. His wife had given it
to him after ten years of marriage. Inside was inscribed, "Where you go
I will go, and where you lodge I will lodge." The gesture of reverence,
which the minister did not rebuff, was eminently right on both sides, for
the air was charged with fidelity.

Christian life is a life of endurance that hopes ultimately to reign. Not
in some distant future but in a final age that has already begun. Can

there be a denial of the love that defines this realm? It is always present as a possibility. But two can play at that. "Of him will the Son of man also be ashamed," said Jesus. The apostolic letter says, by way of para-phrase, "He will also deny us." The hymnodist of those early years then has second thoughts. "Though we be faithless, he remains faithful." The Risen One can no more deny himself than can Israel's God. This saying is sure.

Life goes on; so long as we are in it, it has a way of continuing. An-other day, another week. "Rise and go your way." But this time in a new spirit: "Your faith has made you well."

Faith is a healing of our weakness, a joining of our dividedness, a release from our fetteredness.

If people come away from hearing Bernstein's *Mass* with any refrain on their lips, it is almost invariably, "But you cannot imprison/The word of the Lord."

Those haunting bars are a victory for the music maker and for his lyricist, the author of 2 Timothy.

In the world of sports, they sometimes speak of the "triple crown." Long after the melody has died, will there be a third victory, after that of the two who celebrate the word in song—of a Lord who is faithful, a word that is sure?

The Twenty-second Sunday after Pentecost

Lutheran	Roman Catholic	Episcopal	Presbyterian and UCC
Gen. 32:22–30	Exod. 17:8–13	Exod. 17:8–12	Exod. 17:8–13
2 Tim. 3:14–4:5	2 Tim. 3:14–4:2	2 Tim. 3:14–4:2	2 Tim. 3:14–4:2
Luke 18:1–8a	Luke 18:1–8	Luke 18:1–8a	Luke 18:1–8

EXEGESIS

First Lesson: Gen. 32:22–30. In the ancient Near East, the ford of a river was thought to be an especially dangerous place, since a *jinn* or demon might lurk there to do harm to passersby. But when the nomadic Jacob and his household reached the crossing of the Jabbok, a tributary of the Jordan on the eastern side of the great cleft of the Jordan Valley, all passed over safely except the patriarch himself, who remained alone by the ford without passing over (v. 24).

At first the narrative reports that a man wrestled with him throughout the night, but it is soon apparent that his adversary is really God himself (v. 28). The name "El" is a general name for God or gods in that period, though later tradition was of course to identify the being who wrestled with Jacob as Yahweh (Exod. 3:16; 1 Kings 18:36). It is possible that the Jacob cycle and the Israel cycle were originally separate patriarchal narratives, but in this story the two traditions merge, so that the new name received on this occasion by Jacob is "Israel." Equally important for the tradition incorporated here in Genesis 32 are the struggle between God and Jacob and the fact that Jacob sees God "face to face" (v. 30). In a religion like that of the patriarchs, according to which God is never to be represented by images, it was considered to be an awesome, even a perilous experience to behold God. The dreadful consequences of making contact with the God of Israel are described in connection with the theophany to Moses on Mount Sinai (Exodus 19). In the Jacob story as well, the vision of God brings both revelation and judgment to Jacob: he is designated as the father of the nation, but his fallibility and the awesomeness of coming into the presence of God remain with him in the form of his subsequent lameness.

Jacob's arrogance is evident in his request to know the name of God. Names were believed to be not merely arbitrary designations for distinguishing one person or one member of a species from another, but a means of exercising control over others. God will not disclose his name to Jacob, lest that wily patriarch try to use his power to coerce God into acting in his behalf. The initiative in choosing Jacob and in using him as instrument of the divine purpose remains solely with God, in spite of Jacob's privilege of seeing his face.

Second Lesson: 2 Tim. 3:14–4:5. The writer lays stress on the stability and continuity of the Christian community. From youth upward instruction had grounded the members of the church in matters of faith and practice, especially in Christian interpretation of the Scriptures. At the time these words were written (3:15–16), the Bible of the church consisted solely of the Jewish Bible, probably including all three divisions: Law, Prophets, and other writings (Luke 24:44). It is believed that when these writings are illumined within the church by the Holy

Spirit they exert a multiple effect, achieving instruction in doctrine and morals and developing Christian discipline. The writer is persuaded that it is only through Christian interpretation of the Scriptures that anyone can become adequately equipped for his function within the community (3:17).

The various ministries which the church is to carry out are then briefly sketched (4:2), prefaced by a most solemn reminder of the one in whose name and by whose manifest authority the Christian community has been called into being (4:1). His role is based on his advent into the world, on his having inaugurated the kingdom of God, and will be consummated in the future when he is seen again as judge of all mankind (4:1). The primary task of the church is to proclaim the message of the gospel, but it is to be conveyed by unrelenting use of words that will bring conviction, that will warn the indifferent or the calloused, and it is to be accompanied by careful, patient instruction. Thus conversion by evangelistic methods is not enough; faith must be deepened and confirmed by a wide-ranging program of instruction fitted to the needs of the converts.

The proclaimer of the gospel is to be forewarned, however, that among many members of the community the results of this faithful work will not be enduring. There will be a decided preference for listening to what suits the whims or gratifies the tastes of the hearers. Scorning the traditional patterns for faith and practice, there will be in the near future many who will abandon the rigor of Christian truth in favor of delightful or exciting little tales that caress the ear or inflate the ego. In the face of the impending apostasy the writer calls his readers to stand firm in the faith, to accept persecution and violent opposition, and by proclaiming the gospel to discharge the responsibilities that have been placed upon them as agents of the gospel.

Gospel: Luke 18:1-8a. If this were not a parable but a narrative account or an allegory about God it would create a serious moral problem for the thoughtful reader. It is scarcely praiseworthy that the judge has to be driven by persistence to tend to the needs of a wronged widow or that he "neither fears God nor regards man" (v. 4). Nor does it seem appropriate to suppose that God answers prayer only because his petitioners "bother" him (v. 5). Indeed, the judge is explicitly said to be unrighteous. How to resolve this interpretive difficulty?

Probably the parable was not originally uttered in response to the question about persistence in prayer as a way of guaranteeing results (v. 1). The story may concern an actual case of an indifferent judge who could be moved only by importunity. The point of the parable would be that of arguing from the lesser to the greater. On the one hand there is the careless judge who has no real concern for those whose injustices he is supposed to rectify. But the persistence of the wronged woman, coupled with his own profound annoyance at her maddeningly frequent approaches to him to remind him of her unjust treatment lead him finally to the conclusion that the only way to be rid of her is to settle her case in her favor.

Jesus then would be saying, "If this wretch of a judge can at long last be driven into action, how much more will God respond to your petitions and vindicate you in the face of your adversaries?" The irresponsible judge acted slowly and reluctantly; God will act speedily and with deep concern. Like many of the parables, this is a metaphorical portrait of the gracious nature of God rather than a didactic statement about human actions.

HOMILETICAL INTERPRETATION

Today's scripture readings are about tradition. Genesis tells how Jacob, the supplanter (cf. 25:26), became Israel, the striver with God and men. It was a story told by fathers to sons. The legend explains, if you follow it to the end, why Israelites did not eat a certain joint of meat, a taboo much older than the tale.

2 Timothy pleads for traditional behavior when it recommends reading the Jewish Scriptures. They contain "what you have learned" about salvation through faith in Jesus Christ. The alternatives to sound teaching in the tradition, the letter says, are myths and novelties.

The judge of Luke's parable departs from the tradition of just judgment, but the widow appeals to a tradition equally old: dogged perseverance in pursuit of her rights. The latter proves more durable.

In all these tales and teachings, behavior of long standing is held up for praise; the innovative is repudiated. That is scarcely the mood of the times. Tradition has become a word for stodginess. The innovative gets the foundation grant.

People write books called *Never Trust a God over Thirty* and *We Were Never Their Age.* Everyone knows what they mean.

Thomas Masaryk is credited with having said: "Tradition for us is not the dead hand of the past pressing down the present: Tradition is the covenant of fathers and sons!" The thought is sublime but could be taken as being static. A wit has put it better: "Tradition is having a baby, not wearing your grandmother's hat."

Tradition creates out of elements of the past. It does not put the past on "replay" and leave it there.

Chesterton faulted Tennyson's "Locksley Hall" for celebrating the newly dedicated English railway with the phrase, "the ringing grooves of change." A groove, he said, admits of no change whatever. You progress, but at the price of deadly sameness.

Christianity from the beginning put a high value on tradition. Tradition carries within it, however, the seeds of possible betrayal of the message. The *paradosis* dear to the Christian Fathers was the noun of *paradidomi,* the "handing over" of Jesus in all the betrayal and condemnation texts. The Italians make the same point in two words: *Traduttore traditore,* the translator is a traitor. Passing along can be corrupted into delivering over with terrifying ease.

How does the Christian tell the difference and, more importantly, act on the difference? He looks to what is real in the message, to sound teaching; not to familiar teaching, for much of that can be unsound. He passes along faithfully but also modifies at need, just as a mother does in the womb from the genes she had to work with.

St. Paul was a man committed to tradition. He passed along just what he received, using rabbinic phrasing in his claim (1 Cor. 15:3). The faithful disciple, like a good cistern, does not lose a drop. Yet Paul showed a marvelous disregard for tradition when human need indicated another course. He praised the pastoral principle of the Palestinian churches, where teachers sought support for their services. Then he resolutely boasted that he himself adhered to the opposite principle of self-support.

In another matter, he cited a word of the Lord prohibiting a man and a woman from separating from each other, then proceeded to insert a word of his own—"if she does"—all in the same confident spirit. His principle was clear, and it was Jesus' principle: consider the circumstances. Man was not made for the sabbath, the sabbath was made for man.

Yet neither Paul nor Jesus flouted religious traditions.

The single norm in the NT for heresy is departure from the accepted teaching, that which was handed down. There is truth, however, in the quip which says that the seven last words of a dying church are, "We never did it that way before."

Perhaps the solution is this: total flexibility in customs, total fidelity in teaching.

Try it. You won't like it. You'll find it impossible, so closely are custom and teaching intertwined.

One age's orthodoxy can be another age's heresy. Paul met a challenge he was faced with and taught faith's importance over works; James did the same and pressed for works over faith. *Homoiousios* was a Catholic term fifty years before Nicaea; at that council it became an Arian term. Vincent of Lérins thought he had identified Christian faith in his pithy canon, "What is taught always, what is taught everywhere, what is taught by all." But when it is applied to specific doctrines it can break down. John Henry Newman gave the same matter a good try in his *Essay on the Development of Doctrine.* Its conclusion, on very close examination, proves to be that the surviving doctrines survived.

The church has been torn many times over faithfulness to tradition and departure from it. So have congregations and parishes, religious groups and associations. This is not a religious phenomenon, by any means. Nations and tribes, whole civilizations, have been sundered by deviation from the folkways, the ordered settlements of the past. Sometimes the phenomenon is tragic, yet we have some watchwords of Jesus that favor a break with the past: "No one sews a piece of unshrunk cloth on an old garment. . . . No one puts new wine into old wineskins." The gospel was an important departure from old and honored traditions. All healthy development necessitates such departure. But departure from the gospel itself is nowhere praised. How can the paradox be resolved?

We need to know what is and is not the substance of the gospel to be clung to. Whether the question is one of ethical behavior, democratic institutions, healthful living, or the gospel of Christ, there is always a kernel or core that commands attention. For the Christian there is nothing quite like the gospel, hence the first three examples are analogies —but they are useful ones. We do well to avoid phrases like "unchanging substance" or "undeviating tradition." That which remains the same in every age does so in virtue of adaptation, accommodation to new demands.

Heraclitus said long ago that there is nothing permanent but change. Everyone has said it since then. Whitehead gave the matter serious thought. "The art of progress," he concluded, "is to preserve order amid change and change amid order." The order called for is not always that of logic. More often it is the order of sensibility, feeling, insight. The people who "never did it that way before" did it another way: a familiar way, a comfortable way. They too have rights. They may even be right. At the very least they are convinced of the rightness of their way, and that fact is not unimportant. In their commitment to the familiar they need to be heeded. Chesterton called it counting headstones as well as heads.

Crossing oneself with three fingers or five; adding the phrase in the Creed, "and from the Son," or omitting it; wearing the cotta or the academic gown; declaring the sacraments valid when rightly celebrated or only when by a minister and a recipient in grace. That list is a mixed bag of tradition and traditions that have separated peoples, brought down governments, and left men lying with pikestaffs in their skulls. The same principles can be illustrated with ways of taking up the collection or decorating the sanctuary: no pikestaffs, but the same general outcome. Observe the indiscriminate listing above of gesture and trinitarian theory, vesture and human sanctification. Inconsistent? Mad? No, just the way ordinary humanity manages to see things.

The human psyche is so delicate that it normally cannot separate the emotional and the rational, the cognitive and the conative. It takes on global problems. A proposed formula of faith and a movement of the body in sacred circumstances are all one to most of humankind. The teacher in the name of Jesus Christ—and that includes all of us—needs to remember this. He discloses the deeper reality behind a phrase, a gesture, at his peril. Yet his whole calling is to live perilously, while not scandalizing the "little ones."

Maurice Wiles writes in an epilogue to his book *The Divine Apostle* that the commentators on Paul in the patristic age, being lesser minds and also wishing to systematize the relation of man to God, "tamed" Paul in presenting him. They made him "the domesticated apostle."

We do that all the time with our moralizing, not only of Paul but of

Jesus himself. When we do manage to disclose the message of either one, however tentatively, the wineskins .break. The result is messy for teacher and taught.

Once there was a wrestling match, wrote the author of Genesis. Plucky Israel ("God rules"?) derived its name from it; Israel's eponymous ancestor, who used to be Jacob, acquired a bad limp.

God will vindicate his chosen who cry out to him, like the widow who never gave up.

Salvation is to be found through faith in Christ Jesus, which the Scriptures "have instructed you in since childhood."

Stay persistently with the familiar: old tales, old techniques, old teachings.

Yet: "Behold, I make all things new"; "The old has passed away, the new has come."

How to resolve the two?

Tradition is the ever renewed, hence the ever new. It is the same that always looks different, the risen Christ who is more than a resuscitated corpse.

Walking the path between the old and the new takes all the delicate balance of a conservative radical like Jesus. Ancient India knew the problem and spoke of the "razor's edge."

The Twenty-third Sunday after Pentecost

Lutheran	*Roman Catholic*	*Episcopal*	*Presbyterian and UCC*
Deut. 10:12–22	Ecclus. 35:15b–17, 20–22a	Ecclus. 35:12–14, 16–19	Deut. 10:16–22
2 Tim. 4:6–8, 16–18	2 Tim. 4:6–8, 16–18	2 Tim. 4:6–8, 16–18	2 Tim. 4:6–8, 16–18
Luke 18:9–14	Luke 18:9–14	Luke 18:9–14	Luke 18:9–14

EXEGESIS

First Lesson: Deut. 10:12–22. Here is set forth the essence of the covenant relationship between God and his people, a bond that carries with it both privilege and responsibility. Yet both these aspects are grounded in the nature of God himself rather than arising from arbitrary obligations that he has imposed on his people. He is to be held in awe, but he is also to be loved. His commandments are to be obeyed, all of them, and his purpose is to be served. Yet such obedience is to flow from a commitment of the will ("heart") and of life itself ("soul") to the service of God (10:12).

Out of the vastness of the universe that is his, God has chosen the covenant people for a special relationship to himself. His motivation for doing so was his love for them, not their merit nor any other superior quality of theirs. Given the fact that they are beneficiaries of that love, they are called to commit their wills to his purpose, just as the outward rite of circumcision is an external evidence of belonging to the covenant people (v. 16). The God who deals thus with Israel is both loving and powerful, demanding and gracious. He is above favoritism or bribery. His special concern is with the oppressed and the outcast, so that his love is not a way of feeling but a way of acting in order to meet concretely the needs of mankind (v. 18). His love for Israel is to be the model of their loving action toward others. If God thus continues to be the ground of their awed obedience, of the reliability of their commitments, of their rejoicing, he will also be the guarantor of their destiny (vv. 19–21). From the cluster of nomads camping of necessity on the fringe of the delta of the Nile, God will form a great people, in fulfillment of the promise to Abraham (Gen. 22:17), whose faith made him willing to offer up his own son in response to the command of God.

Second Lesson: 2 Tim. 4:6–8, 16–18. The writer, "Paul," has come to the conclusion that his work is complete, but that God is about to ask of him the greatest of all tests of faith: that he be willing to give his life as a testimony (4:6). He rejoices in retrospect over the challenge and achievement of his striving in behalf of the gospel (4:7). Yet he does not regard death as an end to that enterprise, but as a departure to share in the life of the kingdom of God. There may be delay before that new life is entered upon, but God has already reserved it for him, and when the day comes, it will be his (4:8). Others will share in that reward, whose devotion to the advent of Jesus—God's manifestation in human form (1 Tim. 3:16), the mystery of faith—is such that they also will die a martyr's death and receive the martyr's crown. Indeed the word we translate as "witness" is in Greek *martyros*.

The writer depicts Paul as having abundant reason for having become discouraged or even for abandoning the faith. After his own life of exemplary fidelity to God and his people, at the moment of his trial, no one rallied to his support. None joined his defense. Yet he cannot find it in himself to resent their cowardice; rather, he asks God's forgiveness of them for their lack of the courage of faith. Nevertheless God did not desert Paul in his hour of greatest need, but provided him the strength and eloquence to present his case for the gospel among the Gentiles in the court. So effective was his proclamation of the message that he, for the moment at least, was saved from execution. Whether the "lions" (v. 17) are metaphors for the savage Roman authorities or literal indications of his expectation of being put to death by being torn by wild animals in the arena is impossible to determine. Later tradition reports that he was beheaded, which was a standard mode of execution for Roman citizens. But God is able to deliver even from the evil that is death, and to grant to the faithful victorious participation in his kingdom. The ultimate credit for the fidelity of his witness is thus not accorded to the apostle but to God.

Gospel: Luke 18:9-14. Unlike many of the parables which make their point by an extended metaphor in narrative form (such as the parables of the seed), Jesus here gives a direct and vivid illustration of two ways in which persons may perceive themselves in relation to God.

The Pharisee is conscious of his right to approach God in the temple. He is fully aware of his religious superiority to most others among his fellow creatures. In his heart are no pangs of guilt about overt injustices or violations of the law of God. Indeed his piety exceeds the legal requirements both in the frequency of his fasting and in the base on which he calculates his tithe. What passes for a prayer, therefore, is nothing more than self-congratulation (v.11). It gives no hint of obligation to others and views even obligation to God solely in terms of external, measurable performance. There is no suggestion of such motivation as love, contrition, gratitude, awe. There is only pride of accomplishment, and the implication that God will do well to take notice of a stellar performance of this sort.

By contrast, the tax collector, whose means of livelihood made him religiously and morally suspect and condemned him to hatred and resentment by his fellow Jews as a collaborationist with the Roman overlords, approaches the dwelling place of God in the temple with a deep sense of his own unworthiness. He calls attention to his sins, not his merits. He does not remind God of his pious accomplishments but seeks acceptance in spite of his failures (v. 13). But God does not need man's self-estimate in order to determine his true worth. The man who offers himself as a model of religiosity is due for humiliation, while the man overwhelmed with the sense of his inadequacy and lack of fitness to approach God receives full acceptance (v. 14).

HOMILETICAL INTERPRETATION

There is a street in Rome called Via Bocca di Leone. It is named for a piece of statuary that was once a water fountain, fitted into the porch of a church. Those familiar with the late, late show will perhaps have seen Cary Grant and Audrey Hepburn standing at the lion's mouth which gave the street its name, in an oldie called *Roman Holiday.* She is a princess in disguise, he is a newsman, and true love ultimately triumphs. On the porch just off the narrow street he inserts his hand into the lion's mouth, then quickly withdraws an empty sleeve. It is a superb piece of clowning by an old hand. No pun intended.

The lion of the Bible is not our familiar monarch of the forest but a mountain lion or bobcat. Rescue from its jaws was no figure of speech. The nomad Israelites were familiar with raids on their flocks and herds, and often on their persons. The desert (or "wilderness") was not thought of as the dwelling place of evil spirits for nothing. Foxes and deer were the gentler creatures there. The lions, jackals, and hyenas were another story—a force to be reckoned with by a grazing people who counted their wealth in cattle, sheep, and goats.

The biblical phrase "I was rescued from the lion's mouth" came easily to the author of 2 Timothy, even though this city dweller of the diaspora had probably never seen one. He was a veteran missionary in the Pauline tradition who was trying to convey to a younger man what Paul had been through at imperial hands. The apostle had been deserted by his closest associates but the Lord Jesus always stood by him, giving him the strength to preach the word fully. The Gentiles heard much from Paul that was filled with spirit and power, before he finished the race.

The Greek Christian author uses phrases current in his time, including some from the sports world, as Paul did. "Keeping faith" was already a fixed expression meaning "maintaining a trust." Virgil has Queen Dido saying "I have finished the race." A crown (of righteousness) was the laurel wreath of winners in the track and field events.

The Deuteronomist, centuries before, had been just as alert to the marvel of God's care as the Pauline author. He did not write auto-biographically but in terms of the providence exerted on behalf of the whole people. They went down to Egypt seventy persons and became as numerous as the stars in the heavens. Not everyone appreciated this growth rate, certainly not the Egyptians. But the people had seen marvels ("great and terrible things") that kept them free of the lion's mouth in the long years spent as sojourners.

There was a remarkable figure in this country in the last century, an upstate New York-born slave named Isabella who in 1843 renamed her-self Sojourner Truth. She was an abolitionist lecturer whose six feet of height and remarkable flow of words gave her a commanding platform presence. When she spoke, the hostile crowds listened.

Sojourner Truth. What better name for Israel in her desert days, representing as she did a God of justice who was not partial and who took no bribe? The Deuteronomist lived long after those years of wan-dering but he caught their spirit perfectly. He hammered out a charter of liberties and duties—the terms of the covenant—that his people would never improve on. The circumcised foreskin of a heart no longer stub-born; love and service with all the heart and soul; commandments and statutes to be kept because the Lord had set his heart in love upon the fathers. A God who executes justice for the fatherless and the widow, who gives food and clothing to the sojourner, who has chosen—for all time to come—the descendants of the desert wanderers. Who could fail to be faithful to a God like that?

One of the oldest words used by Christians to describe themselves was *paroikoi*, a biblical term for "sojourners" (the other word to say the same thing is *proselytoi*). We get the word *parish* from the Greek for "sojourner," likewise the word for a parish pastor—in Latin, *parochus*. A cruel irony has made *parochial* synonymous with *narrow* and *confined*, whereas the word belongs to travelers: people on pilgrimage who have no lasting city. With all the gifts of grace that came with Jesus, there was no better statement of the terms of covenant blessing than this. Not even the renewed covenant in his blood gave a clearer reading of the relation between sons and a Father. His chosen descendants grew more numerous still, the Christian believes. The terms were not restricted or altered, only enlarged.

"He is your glory, he, your God, who has done for you those great and terrible things your own eyes have seen."

The eyes of the pious observant in Jesus' parable saw nothing. The inward gaze of the tax gatherer—hated agent of a foreign power—saw everything. This tale can not be bettered as a reading of the Day of Atonement (Yom Kippur). Maimonides wrote in the Middle Ages: "Every man should confess his sins, and turn away from them on *Yom Kippur.*" There is no intention here of connecting this parable with the tenth and last of the Days of Penitence. It is simply that the spirit of the publican was that of this feast. The Confession of Yom Kippur is repeated several times during the day. It involves a cataloguing of no fewer than fifty-six categories of sin. Jews repeat the formula: "For the sin we have committed before thee [stating one of the fifty-six kinds], O God of forgiveness, forgive us, pardon us, grant us remission," and beat their breasts. The publican put all his begs in one ask it: "God, be merciful to me a sinner!"

A strange cynicism among us has resulted in the term *breast-beating,* meaning profitless self-accusation. In a society that repents of nothing but only regrets its boo-boos, any show of repentance can be taken as a reproach. The term *repentance* might indicate that there was something to be sorry for. Hence it stands for a kind of mad masochism such as you find in woolly-headed liberals who think there is something in our national policy to cause us shame, or businessmen who think that the church's response to life's problems has been a meddling in their affairs.

The non-breast-beater-in-principle turns up in Jesus' parable. He stands erect and while he prays "within himself" cannot forego the opportunity to inform the Lord. "As you will have noted in my recent conduct. . . . As my personnel folder will disclose. . . . As I exalt myself in preparation for my inevitable downfall."

The pseudonymous author of 2 Timothy reviews Paul's career and expects a crown of righteousness for him. Preachers over the ages have praised him for doing so. The Pharisee intimates a similar lot for himself and has received a good thumping ever since. We take our lead from Jesus, of course, who did not praise the self-righteous who despised others. We are also predisposed to honor Paul. Are we not, however, inconsistent?

Probably not. Paul did not think ill of anyone who, like him, considered himself righteous in the Lord. He expected all his converts to keep faith, to finish the race just as he did. The Pauline author hints darkly at itching ears and unsound teaching. The publicans of his experience are the steady ones who endure suffering, who do an evangelist's work and fulfill their ministry.

How are we to think of humility, of self-abasement? Dr. Thomas Harris tells us we are a nation of people prone to say "I'm not OK but you're OK." That may be. He is in his office all day long and these are the people he meets. Has he been out in the streets lately, one wonders, in business, in politics, encountering all those healthy psyches that have absolutely nothing to declare? Sin? Sorrow? You've got to be kidding. "I goofed. Everybody does. You can't be right all the time."

The passion to be right is our national obsession. The only sin is not having the facts, not psyching things out—being wrong.

The tax collector did not say he *was* wrong. He said he *did* wrong. He thought it over before God and repented having done what he did.

The Pharisee reflected on his recent activity and saw that it was good. He had heard similar reports about God and came to the temple for an exchange at peer level.

If Israel broke the covenant, the Deuteronomist knew, she could expect to be brought low. Jesus told a tale of two Jews, one who thought he had broken it and another who could not entertain the proposition.

How are we to think of humility? As breast-beating, modern-style? Pulling our psyches to pieces and ending up on the psychiatrist's couch? Or just facing a few facts about ourselves that have not appeared in the newspapers lately?

The Catholic church's Tridentine legislation of 1563 proposes that serious sins be confessed in number and kind if the confession is to be valid. Years ago, in old St. Mary's Church on Wabash Avenue in Chicago, a wheezing voice said to a now long-dead confessor: "Father, I've been a son of a bitch."

Trent lost that round—to the Gospel according to Luke.

The Twenty-fourth Sunday after Pentecost

Lutheran	Roman Catholic	Episcopal	Presbyterian and UCC
Exod. 34:5–9	Wisd. 11:23–12:2	Wisd. 11:23–12:2	Exod. 34:5–9
2 Thess. 1:1–5, 11–12	2 Thess. 1:11–2:2	2 Thess. 1:1–5, 11–12	2 Thess. 1:11–2:2
Luke 19:1–10	Luke 19:1–10	Luke 19:1–10	Luke 19:1–10

EXEGESIS

First Lesson: Exod. 34:5–9. The climax of the series of appearances of God to Moses described in the Book of Exodus occurs in the account of the second giving of the Law, following Israel's gross disobedience in worshiping the calf of gold (Exodus 32). Moses approached God equipped once more with the stone tablets on which the Law was to be inscribed (cf. Exod. 32:15). In a cloud of glory the Lord appeared to him and once more gave Moses his name (cf. Exod. 3:13 ff.), the instrument by which Israel's destiny was to be guaranteed and by which the Israelites could summon God to their aid. Linked with God's name, Yahweh (meaning "he who *is*" or "he who causes to be"), is the character of God which is now disclosed as well (34:6–7).

First to be enumerated are his gracious qualities of mercy and compassion, but especially his fidelity to his covenant promises, which is the chief ground of Israel's relationship to God. From these qualities flows out his forgiveness, which reaches to innumerable members of the community who disobey his commands. But also stressed here is the fact that the consequences of such acts of disobedience are felt not only by those who committed them, but also by successive generations as well. This is a thoroughly understandable factor in human existence, since in any culture and in any age, gross errors create problems which outlast the generation that committed them. Yet Jeremiah was later to criticize those who blamed current difficulties on their parents' generation (Jer. 31:29). No, he said, each generation must accept responsibility for its own misdeeds.

Moses then is depicted as prostrating himself in the presence of Yahweh, asking him to exercise forgiveness and to accept Israel as his covenant people. In doing so Moses acknowledges that Israel is not noted for purity or submissiveness, but for being stubborn and sinful. There is a beautiful irony here: God has already chosen this nation to be his covenant people, in spite of or because of their waywardness, or as might be said, their thoroughgoing humanity. Yet Moses feels obligated to assume nothing, and therefore in genuine humility and contrition in behalf of his people asks God to accept them as his own. They are to be his "inheritance," so that from now on he will be responsible for their destiny.

Second Lesson: 2 Thess. 1:1–5, 11–12. In addressing the churches under his charge, Paul employs a greeting that combines the Greek tradition of his time with the Hebrew tradition of his own heritage. Instead of the Greek commonplace *chairete* ("may you be well") and the Hebrew *shalom* ("peace"), Paul regularly writes "Grace [*charis*] and peace," thus pointing to God's fidelity to his covenant in the gift of grace and the peace that he has effected by his reconciling act in the cross of Christ.

Paul's special joy in the Thessalonians is that they are growing in faith at the very moment that they are undergoing suffering. Perhaps even more remarkable is that their love for one another continues to increase during this time of stress, a circumstance that would in graceless communities merely increase friction and multiply misunderstanding. He has good grounds, therefore, in boasting of the effects of grace in their midst.

One reason that they are able to cope in such a positive way with the difficulties they are experiencing is that their suffering is rightly regarded, not as punishment for misdeeds, but as purifying and maturing them in preparation for entering the kingdom of God. Jesus had stressed the fact that it was necessary for him to suffer (Mark 8:31) without ever explaining why, just as in Isaiah 53 suffering is seen as in some unspecified way bringing benefits to others. And here the trials through which God's people are passing are preparing them for their role in the new age as the worthy people of God.

The initiative in calling them to be members of God's people came from God himself, yet the responsibility lies with them to see that his call achieves its aim in their becoming an obedient and effective instrument of his purpose. The highest objective of all—one that can be achieved only when his people are obedient and effective—is to bring glory to the person of Jesus Christ, through whom the grace of God has been made accessible to faith.

Gospel: Luke 19:1–10. Zacchaeus had nearly everything working against his ever finding a community of acceptance or a religious group that would welcome him. As a tax collector he was collaborating with the hated Romans and was under suspicion by his fellow countrymen of practicing deceit or extortion. The suspicion was seemingly confirmed by the acknowledgment in the Gospel account that he was "rich." In spite of his subsequent protests that he was free of fraud, that he made recompense for any misdeeds, and that he was astonishingly generous (v. 8), the suspicion remains that either he was exaggerating his good works or that he was compensating for his guilt by his generosity.

But in any case, Zacchaeus was the unlikely and unexpected host to the self-inviting Jesus on the occasion of the latter's final journey through Jericho. There would have been religiously safer places, and no one can suspect that it was wealth alone that attracted Jesus to the runty tax collector (v. 3). It was rather to make the point that God's grace does far more than tolerate the outsider and the outcast: it is his nature to extend mercy and grace to those who are most in need. The only prerequisite was that Zacchaeus know that he was in need; that is indicated in his making the effort to "see who Jesus was" (v. 3) by climbing the tree. With no ceremony, Jesus called him down out of the tree, and Zacchaeus responded to the request with understandable haste. In receiving Jesus, he received the reconciling grace of God that Jesus brought. Whether one thinks of "Son of man" as the divinely sent agent of God commissioned to bring in his kingdom (Daniel 7) or as the representative of man before God (Mark 2:27–28), in accepting Jesus, Zacchaeus found acceptance with God and a share in the community of faith stretching back to Abraham.

HOMILETICAL INTERPRETATION

There is a residence in the heart of downtown Philadelphia—behind the Scottish Rite Cathedral and not far from the Schaff Building of the United Church of Christ—which has carved in stone on its lintel the letters *A.M.D.G.* A trip to City Hall or the Historical Society of Pennsylvania might disclose the circumstances of construction of this brick row house. Or a conversation with the oldest inhabitant. It does not much matter. Some dweller was proclaiming his intent of having all passage through that front door be made *ad maiorem Dei gloriam*, "for the greater glory of God." A mezuzah is placed on the doorpost of a Jewish household to invite the same response.

Paul (or the Pauline writer) has a similar hope for the church of Thessalonica: that God may fulfill their every good resolve and work of faith, helping them achieve thereby the glorification of the Lord Jesus. Years ago St. Irenaeus wrote, "The glory of God is enlivened man." That translation does not quite do it but the alternatives are worse: "living man" or "man alive." The reference, of course, is to life in Christ, that *zōē* of the Fourth Gospel which is quite a different matter from *bios*, ordinary animate existence.

The mood of the opening prayer of thanks in 2 Thessalonians is apocalyptic: "When he comes on that day to be glorified in his saints, and to be marveled at in all who believe." The meaning is unmistakable. God's glory made manifest then will spring from a faith life now. In Thessalonica. In Philadelphia—across from the back door of the Hahnemann Hospital where their business is life. *A.M.D.G.*

Jesus' business was life. He came to bring life to everybody, life to anybody. You cannot deduce from Luke's telling of it whether Zacchaeus was a decent man. He was engaged in a lucrative trade, that much is sure, and most lucre is filthy. He traded on the economic weakness of his fellow Jews in the face of a foreign power. Zacchaeus gave gifts to the poor. He tried to set right the daily injustices that were his stock in trade. The king in Thurber's "Thirteen Clocks" says: "Everyone has his little weaknesses. Mine is, I'm wicked." Zacchaeus defrauds. Then he makes contributions. Both on a regular basis.

The Egged tour bus, the national transport service of Israel, makes its dusty way through modern Jericho. It is not ancient Jericho, which is nearby. The guide makes that clear. You get to see both within a short space. In the modern town you are shown an ancient tree, gnarled and symmetrical, along one of the main streets. Tradition has it, the guide announces in toneless respect, that a certain Zacchaeus climbed that tree to get a better look at Jesus. The people of Palestine have always been obliging in that way: when Queen Helena came, when the crusaders came, when the Russian pilgrims came. Anything anyone wanted to see, the locals found for them. For the glory of Allah? Elohim? But why disappoint pious hope?

Salvation came on that day to Zacchaeus's house.

"When he comes on that day to be glorified in his saints. . . ."

"The Lord, a God merciful and gracious . . . keeping steadfast love for thousands. . . ."

Always it is a visitation. Always it is *hesed ve emeth*, "steadfast love and faithfulness." These Hebrew words appear in Greek in John's prologue as "grace and truth." Such is God's visitation in Jesus Christ answering to the grace of the law—"grace upon grace." Péguy put it well: "And then I am expected to condemn them. An easy business! / I am supposed to judge them. We all know how those judgments end up, and all those sentences. / *A certain man had two sons.* It always ends with embraces. / (And the father crying more than anybody else.)"

The Lord puts a bold face on things with Moses the second time around at Sinai. The children's children will pay for the sins of the fathers. After all, this is a stiff-necked people. Everybody has his little shortcomings. Theirs is iniquity. And the Lord's? Failure of nerve. "Forgiving transgression and sin." And crying more than anybody else.

Jesus' business was life. *Salvation*, read in Hebrew, means saving your skin—or having it saved for you. Read in Greek it translates, "receiving the life of your savior-god." As Luke put the word on Jesus' lips, it surely meant both. He came to bring life to the sons of Abraham—who knew its terms well in the covenanted land. He came to bring life to the Greeks—everyone else, that is, who lived by Alexander's legacy and knew life as it came in the cultic mysteries. "I must stay in your house today." "O that today you would hear his voice! Harden not your hearts. . . ."

The hardened heart chooses death when it is offered life. It does not accept the invitation, it will not come down. Small of stature, it compensates by climbing. It peers down in curiosity but makes no haste. It will not receive life or him who offers it—joyfully or any other way. With life and death held out to it, the sclerotic heart chooses death.

Accustomed to flying missions with impunity, these Air Force officers [the B-52 crews] appeared more the products of their machines than of themselves. Seven days aloft, and until a few days ago seemingly safe in their highly automated aircraft, such crewmen see neither the faces of individuals below nor, even, the inanimate targets they carpet bomb. "Sometimes at night you can see flashes from the bombs dropped by the planes ahead of you," a co-pilot told me. Mindful of the $8 million his Stratofortress costs, one pilot remarked that he thinks of "expensive plowing" when briefing officers display photographs of B-52 destruction. (In South Vietnam alone, our Air Force, so far, has plowed an area the size of Massachusetts.)

Briefings are based on intelligence estimates that often lack detail, one

pilot said. Thus, when airmen learn of "enemy casualties" they have in-
flicted, the estimates do not differentiate between military and civilian
victims. Occasionally, briefings are enlightened by a touch of humor. A
pilot told of one briefing officer who informed a crew, "Yesterday, you
guys wiped out 600 people, two bikes, and a camel. . . ."

Discussing a routine drop of thirty tons, a bombardier who has flown
230 missions told me, "Pressing the button is a mechanical thing, a part
of my job. But I will say this: I'm sure glad when it's over and done with.
It means we can head home without looking for an alternative target. That
could delay us forty minutes, which is a lot, considering it's a twelve-hour
trip from Guam." [Daniel Lang, "Going to Work over Ground Zero"]

It is not these officers who have chosen death. They are part of a people that has. Not only in Southeast Asia. On streets where junkies lie in
doorways. On highways, with maimed bodies sprawled around. On death
row. In youthful gunfire. In problem pregnancies.

Every single one of these cases can be argued. What cannot be argued
is that we are not talking here about life. Or if so, we are talking about
the life of survivors surrounded by death. A better life for the living—
picking their way through the corpses.

A people needs to worry about choosing death. It gets to feel at home
with it, more comfortable than with life. It frames arguments to justify
death—always in terms of life. A better life for Aryan survivors, for the
healthy, for the young, for the democratic, for the proletariat, for the
lighter skinned.

The Greeks had a word for it. Necrophilia: "love of death."

"The Son of man came to seek and save the lost." The lost are not our
familiar categories of sinners but the living dead, the lovers of death. At
first these are the deaths of others but gradually, inevitably their own.

There was a French film of twenty-five or more years ago called *For-
bidden Games*. The children began by burying birds with full *pompes
funèbres*. Cats and dogs came next. More and more they entered into the
spirit of the thing. And then, one day. . . .

Another movie from that same country and time, entitled *We Are All
Murderers*, told of a priest chaplain in Paris who innocently supposed
that the only reason he could have been assigned to the jail was to bring
the guillotining to an end. A prologue to the film centers on a street
urchin in the resistance, now in a death cell. "They put a gun in his
hand, taught him how to shoot, and told him to kill for the liberation of
la patrie. Then, some men signed a piece of paper. But no one remem-

bered to tell the boy. He kept on killing and did not know why they brought him here."

If you read the books sacred to Christians, you learn from them that they are not called to be death merchants. A covenanted people like their fathers, they are told to choose life. Their Master was a life-giver. Yet they kill. For peace, for God, for homeland.

For their own greater glory, in the name of which all things are permitted.

The Twenty-fifth Sunday after Pentecost

Lutheran	Roman Catholic	Episcopal	Presbyterian and UCC
1 Chron. 29:10–13	2 Macc. 7:1–2, 9–14	Job 19:23–27	1 Chron. 29:10–13
2 Thess. 2:16–3:5	2 Thess. 2:15–3:5	2 Thess. 2:15–3:5	2 Thess. 2:15–3:5
Luke 20:27–38	Luke 20:27–38	Luke 20:27, 34–38	Luke 20:27–38

EXEGESIS

First Lesson: 1 Chron. 29:10–13. For centuries after the Israelite tribes infiltrated the land of Canaan, their places of worship consisted of local sacred spots, such as Shechem or Bethel. At one or the other of these holy sites, the symbol of Yahweh's presence in their midst was the portable shrine that had gone with them through the years of desert wanderings. In uniting the northern and southern tribes of Israel under his sole authority, David also provided a new capital city, Jerusalem, and made provision for a single permanent place of worship: the temple on Mount Zion. Although it was not actually built until the time of Solomon, David's successor, David himself is credited by the writer of Chronicles with making ample provision for its construction, and his example evoked generosity on the part of the people as well.

In anticipation of the preparation of the new shrine of Yahweh, David addressed God in solemn words that expressed Israel's sense of dependency on God for all that she was and had. In pronouncing the blessedness of Yahweh, David was merely declaring in the presence of God and his people what the nature of Israel's God is and why it is appropriate to honor him. His sovereign purpose arches over all of time, so that his will is supreme from of old to the farthest horizon of the future. His relationship to his people is that of father, implying depth of concern and love, as well as strictness of discipline. He alone is the possessor of true greatness; all authority—even that of the king—rests with him and derives from him. Awe that the subjects might feel in the presence of their ruler is as nothing compared with the fearful yet fascinating mystery of the nature of God himself, invisibly but powerfully present in the sanctuary. All of Israel's triumphs over enemies are to be credited to him, and what grandeur the nation possesses is his gift alone. "The kingdom" is not to be equated with the territory under David's control, but is an expression of God's rule over the whole of his creation, for which David is no more than temporary agent.

David then confesses that all that he possesses, all the honor that accrues to him as ruler over Israel, all the authority that he exercises, even the fact that he is king at all—all comes from God and is bestowed by him in his grace on his chosen instrument. Thus aware of his status, David has no place for boasting, but only for gratitude.

Second Lesson: 2 Thess. 2:16–3:5. In writing to the faithful at Thessalonica, Paul offers prayer to God in their behalf. His petition is addressed to God, who is the source of encouragement and confidence in the midst of difficulties and opposition, and to Jesus Christ, who by God's grace has become the instrument through whom the gospel has become a reality for faith. Paul prays that through the Father and the Son their dedication to serve God may be confirmed and their effectiveness in doing so may be increased.

But he also asks that they join in prayer in his behalf, especially as he sees hostility mounting and the work of the Adversary increasingly manifest. He has no doubt about what the gospel can effect: the Thessalonian church is itself testimony that the word of God can overcome opposition and accomplish its objectives. But he does not want to see the speedy spread of the gospel hindered by the successful schemes of its human and demonic opponents, who, lacking faith, want to deny to others the privilege of hearing it proclaimed. His confidence does not rest in the persuasiveness of preaching or in his skill in evangelistic organizing, but in the God whose word he preaches. He is the source of power; his fidelity guarantees the effectiveness of the proclamation; his strength is sufficient protection against all opposition.

Paul is therefore confident in the Thessalonians as well, because he knows that their reliance is on God. They will accept the apostle's instructions as God's commands, and will perform them willingly and effectively. Finally, he returns to his request in their behalf, which is that God by his Spirit will continue to bend their wills toward two objectives, by which his expectations concerning them can alone be achieved: (1) love toward God corresponding to his love for them in giving his Son, and (2) their faithful endurance for the sake of Christ in a response of gratitude for his faithfulness unto death in their behalf.

Gospel: Luke 20:27–38. Although precise knowledge about the beliefs of Sadducees is scant, they apparently did not believe in the Jewish doctrine of the resurrection, primarily because it was not taught in the five books of Moses, which alone they regarded as authoritative Scripture. In order to reduce the doctrine to absurdity, they told an imaginary story about a series of seven brothers who, in obeying the levirate law of marriage (Deut. 25:5), successively took as wife the same woman. The question was then to whom she would belong in the age when the dead were brought back to life.

Jesus' response to this challenge was to reject their basic premise that life in the new age was simply a resumption of life as it is experienced in this age. While conscious personal existence is implied in the age of resurrection, the conditions of personhood in this age, such as marital and familial relationships, are wholly changed. Humanity in that setting is no longer subject to earthly limitations, Jesus seems to be saying.

Then the argument shifts to what can only seem to the modern reader of Scripture to be a strange passage on which to base an argument in support of the doctrine of the resurrection. The point of referring to Yahweh as the God of three successive generations of patriarchs, Abraham, Isaac, and Jacob, may be to indicate that God is not subject to temporal limitations, but is the contemporary of every age of man. Or it may be implied that in spite of the deaths of the patriarchs, Yahweh *is* their God, and continues to be so even though by human perspectives these men of old no longer exist. The result in either case would be the same. The patriarchs have not passed from God's eternal purpose even though they have died, nor is he any less their God for their earthly lives being at an end. The service of Israel's God is not the worship of ancestors or the anachronistic preservation of an outworn faith: it is the celebration of the God who is alive, and whose faithful servants have not passed from his purpose because they have passed through death. He remains the ground and the goal of their lives.

HOMILETICAL INTERPRETATION

When David is described as blessing the Lord in the assembly, upon the completion of the fund drive to build the temple, we listen with ease. That is something we can do. We have done it many times over. Freewill offerings, given with a whole heart; gold and silver, bronze, iron, and precious stones by the carload; the treasury of the house of the Lord—all these details are the context of today's first reading, a hymn of praise to God who, in his power and might, gives his people riches and honor and strength. In a word, building is that praise of God which we know best.

Is all the building done to give praise to God? As they say in the Romance languages, "It is able to be."

Medieval France praised God that way in a century of cathedral-building—1140 to 1240—the like of which the world has never seen. All, or almost all, the cathedrals were dedicated to Mary. Bishops were chosen, abbots elected, deans of cathedral chapters named with but a single qualification: they could finish the job. The job was a higher spire than the next town, a handsomer facade, a larger unsupported arch, a higher clerestory. All to the glory of God. "God" was spelled variously as Amiens, Évreux, Chartres, Noyon, Senlis.

Let us make no mistake. Every pastor who has ever lived has a touch of Solomon or Abbot Suger of St.-Denis in his heart. He hopes to build the ultimate earthly house of God.

There were occasional tragedies. After mass one All Saints Day in Beauvais, there was an ominous shower of stones from the *flèche* to the floor below. It became a cascade, then a roar as all came tumbling down, this short-lived, highest spire in France.

Everyone has heard of the contest in Renaissance Italy, where Michelangelo's cupola of St. Peter's Basilica in Rome outstripped the Duomo of Florence in diameter by a yard or two. What came tumbling down in St. Peter's was not masonry but the religious unity of Europe.

God has been splendidly housed since Solomon's time but often at a high price. David, who planned but never built, looks wiser than his son in this matter.

In the outlook of ancient Israel, Jesse lived in David and his victories, David lived in Solomon and his splendor. Jesus has a different mentality, that of the post-Maccabean world. For him, all live to God (Luke 20:38), not in the survival of a people or the deeds of offspring, but all live and will live again in the flesh.

The resurrection of the dead was the keystone in the arch of Pharisee theology. The conviction was that God would vindicate the saints—individually and in person. It was an apocalyptic concept, of course. The risen dead were to live in a new aeon of peace and security. Any notion of reliving the life of the present sinful age was absent. What or how the new existence would be was hidden from the visionaries who conceived it. But none of this deterred them from painting word pictures that tried to convey the reality of a continuing life.

Life, for the Jew, was not life if it was not total. Either the creature man lived again in body and soul or he did not live. Any other view of survival was a contradiction in terms.

The Sadducees viewed the notion crassly and ridiculed it. Their conception was such that it deserved to be ridiculed. Conjugal rights for a *ménage* of eight provide a strain on the liveliest imagination. People have been having fun with the notion of a risen life ever since.

The whole business is mythical, they say, thinking thereby to dismiss it. The whole business is mythical, said the Pharisees, and after them the Christians, thinking thereby to retain it. When myths are taken literally, reified, they are destroyed. The truth of poetry cannot survive such handling. A myth means more and less, always, than it says. The more of "resurrection in the body" is the incapacity to die. The less is that piece of imagery about living like the angels, which explains the obscure through the more obscure.

Jesus' brisk reply to Sadducee scoffers had this merit: it knew that a God of life was not a God of bones and ashes. All who are or ever have been live to him. The just are sons of God, a progeny that rises up to life rather than goes down to the dust.

Jesus was not resigned to the shutting away of loving hearts in the hard ground. He knew how elegant and curled the blossom was, the roses they had gone to feed. But he did not approve, and he was not resigned.

"That the dead are raised, even Moses showed. . . . The Lord is not God of the dead, but of the living; for all live to him."

Patristic theology did a strange thing with one of today's Lucan verses. It put it in the service of a celibate life, an ascetical practice that had risen elsewhere than in the Bible. The NEB translates the aorist perfect passive participle of v. 35 correctly: "those who have been judged worthy." The RSV with its "those who are accounted worthy" is closer to the Latin Vulgate, which rendered it as future: *digni habebuntur*. You can see the confusion. Luke has Jesus saying that those who have been found worthy in the judgment will not be living ordinary lives of sex and marriage in the future. In the new age, life will be different. But if you take the participle as present or future, it can give the sense that those who abstain from sex and marriage in this age will be in some special way "sons of the resurrection." The celibate mentality, to which Jerome contributed so heavily in the West, seems to have influenced his translation. All that the evangelist says is that we can expect the conditions of the new aeon to be quite different from those of the present. "Equal to angels" is Luke's special contribution. Mark and Matthew have "like angels," meaning somehow quite different.

The faith of Christians about life in the risen body is that individual existence will continue but with marvelous differences that cannot be spelled out. St. Paul gives the appearance of spelling them out in detail (cf. 1 Cor. 15:35–54; 2 Cor. 4:16–5:10), but when you read him with care you see that all he says is: "More life; the same person, but different."

The Gospels are filled with mention of the second temple. So is the Book of Acts. Jesus is frequently found there as, later, are his disciples. But the antitemple sentiment that marked the Judaism of the times is never far below the surface. It is not an outright rejection of the temple such as you find in the Qumrân scrolls, but it is there. The temple "built with hands" will be replaced by a temple "not built with hands," which turns out to be Jesus' risen body. Every Jew, whether he followed the Nazarene or not, had to work out some solution to the shocking mystery of the destruction of the temple in A.D. 70. The solution of the Christians was that Jesus' risen body now in glory was the central shrine of their faith and devotion. They attempted no building, they centered their faith on no particular edifice or piece of ground for just this reason. Jesus

Christ, the firstborn from the dead, was the archetype of a risen progeny —"sons of the resurrection." Private homes were the gathering places of believers in him. No temple or synagogue was needed since the center of blessedness was the body of Christ, which "you are" (1 Cor. 12:27).

It would be easy to bemoan the construction of the first Christian church but wiser to omit such lamentation. The first church known to us was part of a private house, dating to 232, in the frontier fortress of Dura-Europos on the Euphrates, the furthest corner of the Roman Empire. It was excavated in 1934 and has been painstakingly reconstructed at Yale. A nearby synagogue, decorated with dozens of unexpected Jewish pictures, has yielded its treasures to the museum at Damascus. The phenomenon of church-building was bound to happen, if only to ensure a gathering place and to protect worshipers against the elements. In itself this is no scandal. Sacred edifices gladden the human heart. They can also give glory to God, if that motive lay behind their construction or lies behind their use. The question is, do these edifices build up or tear down the temple of living stones? Do churches help or hinder the life of the church?

Frequently the question of Judas is put: "Why was this ointment not sold . . . and given to the poor?" Aside from its parentage, the argument has a deeper flaw. The poor seldom see the money that does not go into churches. By and large, the people who build the churches give to the poor. The rich tend to do neither.

The "eternal comfort and good hope" that 2 Thessalonians is speaking about (2:16) is none other than the mystery of Christ. God has acted already. He has raised up his Son whose body is a temple not built with hands. You can miss the meaning of the mystery, erecting a spire of Beauvais or a dome of St. Peter's instead. Or you can accept the mystery *and* build spire and dome—for the right reasons. The two do not exclude each other.

What is mutually exclusive is looking to the work of human hands for strength and protection against evil (cf. 2 Thess. 3:3). The Lord's command is not kept by way of any such recourse.

Comfort, hope. Everyone needs them, the more especially as the temple of the body crumbles and those we love go down into the dust. Who lives again in the body, and how? What *does* happen to the woman of seven husbands?

The usual form that question takes concerns the woman of two or three husbands. What, exactly, is her hope? What is anybody's hope? Not an eternal marriage bed; the Sadducees had that much straight. Our hope is personal existence, like that of the risen Christ, in circumstances entirely new.

The Twenty-sixth Sunday after Pentecost

Lutheran	*Roman Catholic*	*Episcopal*	*Presbyterian and UCC*
Mal. 4:1–2a	Mal. 4:1–2a	Mal. 4:1–2a	Mal. 3:16–4:2
2 Thess. 3:6–13	2 Thess. 3:7–12	2 Thess. 3:7–12	2 Thess. 3:6–13
Luke 21:5–19	Luke 21:5–19	Luke 21:5–19	Luke 21:5–19

EXEGESIS

First Lesson: Mal. 4:1–2a. Like Amos (5:18 ff.), Malachi warns that the Day of the Lord will not be merely a day of deliverance and vindication for the righteous. For the disobedient it will be a time of judgment and destruction. Those who are to be consumed by the fire of divine wrath are in the first instance those who are arrogant. This quality is described in Genesis 3 as the basis of man's estrangement from God: seeking to be like God in knowledge and power, man becomes alienated and guilty, fleeing at the approach of God, clothing himself in leaves and flimsy excuses. Whether the other evildoers are differentiated from the arrogant matters little, since all will be consumed like the dried grass and stubble in a field. So fierce will be the heat of God's judgment that even the roots that remain in the ground will be destroyed. The agent in this destruction will be God himself, here designated by his ancient title "Yahweh of armies," though here his enemies are the proud and disobedient among his own people, not the nations hostile to Israel. The day when this fierce anger is to vent itself is not remote, so that Malachi's hearers must prepare now if they are to escape the judgment.

Destruction is not inevitable, however. God has a different fate in store for those who honor him as God, acknowledging his name and seeking to do his will. The image under which the redemptive instrument of God is depicted is one which stands in sharpest contrast to the destructive fire of judgment. Indeed, the speed with which a fire would race across a Palestinian field was in large measure the result of the climatic conditions there, by which the scorching sun dries up the fields in late spring once the growing season is over. The brief period when the land is green, from the end of the winter rains when the crops spring up to the time when the fields are once again drab and brown, is no more than two or three months. But in Malachi's picture the "sun" which rises does not desiccate; it heals. Pictured here as the source of light and life, this "sun" establishes God's intended order in the earth, it brings light to a people in darkness (Isa. 9:2), and hence heals and redeems rather than working judgment. The benefits of God's saving light are experienced only by those who fear his name; for the rest the prospect remains that of fearful judgment.

Second Lesson: 2 Thess. 3:6–13. Christians in every age have fallen prey to the foolish notion that if they are concerned about spiritual matters they can be completely casual about their other obligations. As one wag phrased it, "They are so heavenly-minded that they are no earthly good." Among the Thessalonians there were Christians of precisely this sort. Basking in their newfound freedom in the gospel, or concentrating solely on the joys of the age to come, they lost sight completely of present obligations to serve in the church and to assume their share of the remunerative work that made possible the carrying on of the church's mission.

Not only does Paul condemn such irresponsibility, he warns the faithful to avoid contact with persons of this indolent variety. The tradition of assuming part of the work load in behalf of the whole community was so firmly fixed as already to be described as a "tradition," as much so as the gospel itself was handed down as tradition (1 Cor. 15:3). Paul could offer himself as an example of a believer who took on his share of the work. He did not sponge on others, taking advantage of their generosity in order to devote himself to "spiritual" matters. He took on gainful work—according to the tradition in Acts 18:3 he was a tentmaker or leather worker—so that he could buy his own food and be in no way financially dependent on others.

His regulation for the churches was unambiguous: Christians were to contribute labor and presumably a part of their earnings as well so that the work of the community could move ahead. Community consisted not in a feeling of togetherness but in the concrete fact of sharing in work and means for the common good and the community's witness. Lazy Christians, presuming on the sweat of others to provide them the necessities of life, are solemnly rebuked and exhorted to assume their share. Hard work is a corollary of faith.

Gospel: Luke 21:5–19. When some of his followers were dazzled by the splendor of the temple—and indeed its glistening limestone and gleaming gold made it one of the most spectacular structures of its epoch —Jesus predicted that it would be destroyed. By A.D. 70 it did lie in ruins, pulled down by the Roman armies under Titus, after a yearlong siege had led to the capture of Jerusalem and the pillaging of the temple treasures, as depicted in the reliefs on the Arch of Titus in Rome.

In response to the request to indicate the signs that would indicate that the fall of Jerusalem was about to occur, Jesus is reported as turning rather to the more immediate question about the cost of discipleship. The persecution of the faithful will take place in a context of international and even cosmic disturbances. War, plagues, famines will sweep over the earth in the time of the end of the age. But before that series of events takes place (v. 12), the troubles will fall upon the Christians themselves, who will be subjected to harassment, trial, and interrogation before both civil and religious authorities, as a consequence of their identification with Jesus as the Christ.

Far from regarding these difficulties as a sign that God has abandoned them, they are to see their situation as an opportunity for Christian testimony in high places. It will be unnecessary for them to plan in advance how they will defend themselves in these pagan and religious courts; God will provide insight and eloquence in the moment of trial, so that the testimony of their adversaries will be effectively refuted. But for all the effectiveness of their defense, it will not prevail: so fierce will be the opposition to their witness for Christ that family and ethnic loyalties will be swept aside, giving way to betrayals by parents and relatives. Some will suffer martyrdom, and all will encounter hatred for their testimony to Jesus. But fidelity will be rewarded, and all will be preserved—whether by faithful life or death—to enter the life of the age to come.

HOMILETICAL INTERPRETATION

The picture of a final conflagration which will achieve judgment by what it consumes and what it spares derives from the Zoroastrian tradition. "The day" is *ha yom Yahweh*, the day of the Lord, understood in the apocalyptic tradition to be a day of vindication for the just but destruction for the wicked. Matching the fire that destroys will be the fire that restores, "the sun of justice with its healing rays [RSV, 'wings']."

Mithraism, likewise Persian in its origins, featured the disc of the sun with its emergent rays. In a later period than that of the fifth-century book of Malachi, Roman diffusion of this Eastern cult featured the sun as *sol invictus*. The unconquerable sun was at its apogee in the winter solstice, but not for long. Immediately after December 21 it began its climb back to the center of the sky, its diminished strength restored with each passing day. The Christians called Jesus Christ *sol iustitiae*, from the Vulgate rendering of Malachi 4:2. He was God's righteousness, the bearer of light and warmth to a people locked in the winter of death and sin. The feast of the Nativity was initiated in the first quarter of the fourth century at Rome to counter the Saturnalia of the solstice—the only major Christian feast to originate in the West.

Weariness in well-doing (2 Thess. 3:13) is a temptation in any season but especially as the year wanes and winter comes on. The sun was admired in the ancient world for its invincible spirit. It would not be downed. Just at the point of its least influence it began the long, daily march up the sky. St. Paul in 2 Thessalonians makes a similar recommendation to the Macedonian believers. Their energies must not flag, least of all on some false theological principle of a victory won or a parousia assured. The Christian misconceives Paul's teaching about the end if he supposes that it can be permitted to paralyze human effort.

The Pauline dependence on apocalyptic imagery is large, if we take the two Thessalonian letters alone as evidence. It has been questioned how a congregation of largely Gentile or even proselyte makeup could have been so responsive to the Jewish imagery of his first letter—if such was the sequence of composition—as to create a climate of inaction, even apathy. We cannot know. Powerful preaching does strange things, sometimes in directions other than those intended.

The worker, the achiever in the apocalyptic of Malachi, is fire. It will destroy the evil and heal the good. Paul yields to no one in his certainty of the coming of the day of Christ but he knows that there are some things that certainty cannot achieve. Among them is earning a livelihood. The assured quality of future judgment does nothing to allay idleness. It may even foster it. Religious enthusiasm, in other words, can have side effects that are harmful to the ordinary business of living.

In George Orwell's allegory *Animal Farm*, Moses the tame raven was not only a spy and a talebearer but also a clever talker. He claimed to know of the existence of a mysterious country called Sugarcandy Mountain, to which all animals went when they died. It was situated beyond the clouds; there, it was Sunday seven days a week. The animals hated Moses because he told tales and did no work, but some of them believed in Sugarcandy Mountain.

St. Paul was interested in an encounter "somewhere up in the sky," to use Orwell's phrase. It turned out to be, for him, a handy borrowing of the Danielic Son of man theme. The latter figure was a mysterious human-angelic being who would come "upon" or "with" clouds (depending on whether one followed the Septuagint version or Theodotion). Paul's commitment to the literal reality of any such imagery can be presumed slight but his certainty of being "with Christ" was total. Meantime, he was the most non-Orwellian creature in the barnyard in his desire to avoid becoming an economically nonproductive unit. Paul was literally obsessed with the ideal of self-support, even though he knew his rights under another tradition (cf. 2 Thess. 3:9). Persons so attentive to the future that they had no time for this world's business earned Paul's contempt. He suspected them thoroughly. They were his Moses-like ravens who told tales (his word is *periergazomenoi*, "busybodies").

Late first-century Palestinians told tales too—not those of Paul's earlier busybodies but real tales of the way the siege of Jerusalem had taken place at Roman hands. The basic facts were gruesome enough. To them were added rationales in explanation. In Christian circles, these were put in Jesus' mouth in the form of prophecy. Luke's special use of Marcan and Q material centered on the fidelity of community members in time of persecution. They would appear before "kings and governors," Luke's term for the Jewish and Roman authorities alluded to in his trial narrative and the Book of Acts. They would be given "a mouth and wisdom," a trace of his motif of the prophetic character of the Elijah-like Jesus. The faithful witness will know how to testify in time of challenge. He need not think out his defense beforehand.

Luke bears the burden, in scholarly circles, of having been the first NT writer to miss the eschatological urgency of Jesus' message. He is the calm theorist of "salvation history," the man who has come to terms with a settled life for the church, the first proponent of "early Catholicism." In none of these designations is he being praised.

To be sure, Luke missed a lot if the only value is the primitive spirit of the tradition. Unfortunately for him, he did not live in the earliest age of church life. He had access to an apocalyptic message but he tempered it to his readers' capacities—when indeed he gave evidence of comprehending it himself. In a word, he adapted a message delivered in Hebraic form to a Greek culture which, like the man himself, might not have known what to make of it in that form.

The problem posed by Luke's Gospel is far older than Luke. The Deuteronomist had the same problem with respect to Mosaic-era material, the Chronicler with the reminiscences of the court historians of the kings of Judah. Do you tell a story "straight" and leave your readers mystified, or do you modify it in terms of what you consider their needs and capacities? How best do you communicate in matters of great importance?

The biblical fundamentalist, the doctrinal fundamentalist, the constitutional fundamentalist are all content with repeating materials from the past. No interpretation, no accommodation, no hermeneutical perspective. Whether it is comprehensible or not, a world view out of the past is considered to be available to people of later ages in its original form.

The community called "church" has the problem constantly of making sense out of ancient materials. Take the present case. The waning church year has but two weeks to run. A tradition has been inherited whereby its final weeks and days have been made the symbol of the last epoch. The difficulties are twofold, at the very least. Christian liturgy originated in the northern hemisphere where November meant the onset of winter, at a time when the church calendar was as significant as the civil in people's lives. Liturgy is symbolic action from first to last, and although Jewish apocalypticism was not a mode of thought in the fourth century through the seventh, similar ritual and cultic conceptions were.

We live in an age when none of the postulates of Malachi or the NT authors employing him can be assumed as meaningful in the culture. There are exceptions, of course. The fans of Velichovsky, von Däniken, and Lindsey cannot get enough of cosmic catastrophe, apocalyptic intervention. To these enthusiasts, the church's acceptance of such themes seems pallid at best. The ordinary citizen, meanwhile, has been so affected by the empirical and the technological, so little touched by poetic imagery, that much of the Bible including its prosaic portions seems like so much moonshine to him.

Yet the makers of lectionaries, the lectors, and the preachers go bravely from one season to the next proclaiming a day burning like an oven which will destroy the wicked like stubble. *Stubble!* Who can define it, out on the sidewalk after church? Earthquakes and famines, pestilence and terror. Who can read these signs? More importantly, in what sense are they signs?

The literalists in our midst increase, but that can scarcely be called gain. The gullible who call their gullibility faith are in an ideal position to be gulled and to lose all faith. Jesus Christ is as imperiled as the pilot of an Unidentified Flying Object, the charioteer at the reins of a span of celestial stallions. The whole matter can end in absurdity unless the preacher rescues it.

The waning year: perennial sign of flagging powers, death overtaking life, the frozen earth, torrential rains. Not only is the sun at its lowest angle; so is the human spirit. There is weariness in well-doing. The rat race; an extra pitcher of martinis; bills for school tuition; roof repair; rumors of a Christmas bonus thoroughly scotched. Who needs pestilence and terror? The dull grey reality of life will do quite well—or ill—enough.

The accommodations of a great theme attempted above will be found by many to be flawed. "That's not the way the blahs hit the people in this town. They're busy drinking boilermakers to face the production line on Monday. They're. . . ."

All right. Work it out any way you please. Just remember that it's a contest that is being described between all that is energy, light, and right-doing, and the demonic, dark places in the human spirit.

The Last Sunday after Pentecost, Christ the King

Lutheran	Roman Catholic	Episcopal	Presbyterian and UCC
Jer. 23:2–6	2 Sam. 5:1–3	Jer. 23:2–6	Job 23:1–7
Col. 1:13–20	Col. 1:12–20	Col. 1:12–20	1 Cor. 15:54–58
Luke 23:35–43	Luke 23:35–43	Luke 23:35–43	Luke 6:39–45

EXEGESIS

First Lesson: Jer. 23:2–6. Speaking in the name of the God of Israel, Jeremiah denounces the leaders of the people who harm and disperse the covenant community rather than devote themselves to ministering to its needs and uniting its members. Even in the hour of unprecedented danger, when the nation was about to be carried off into exile, or perhaps had in part already been led away into captivity in Babylon, the leaders of Judah were interested only in exploiting their positions of power for personal gain. The prophet warns that God will bring them to judgment for their misdeeds and for neglect of their pastoral role.

In the time to come, beyond the impending catastrophe of the exile, God will himself become the shepherd of the flock of faith, calling them out of exile in Babylon and from other lands where they have been scattered, increasing their numbers and enlarging the covenant community. New leaders will be appointed, and unlike their predecessors, these will faithfully discharge their duties. Accordingly, the people will be ministered to, their needs supplied, their minds freed from anxiety, the members preserved from evil. The guarantee of this new epoch of deliverance is the word of God himself.

In the new age that is coming God will execute his will among his people through a new Son of David, the properly constituted heir of the kingdom. Unlike many of the kings of Israel and Judah, he will deal wholly in accord with the divine will, and will create a harmonious and responsible pattern of relationships within the community. Thus he will bring into reality the ideals of Israelite society which, though set forth in the Law, have never yet been achieved. The justice that he administers will not be detached and dispassionate application of laws, but will effect the shaping of men and society so that human relationships will be characterized by responsibility, by peace, by mutual concern, by compassion.

The benefits of the new order will be extended to both Judah and Israel, the northern group of tribes that had been led into captivity by the Assyrians nearly a century and a half earlier. But Jeremiah declares that the whole of the nation will be restored; all twelve tribes will dwell in peace and prosperity in the epoch to come. All will acknowledge that the sole agent by which the oppressed have been released, those unjustly treated have been vindicated, those ground down in slavery have been set free, is "Yahweh who sets matters right," the Lord, our righteousness.

Second Lesson: Col. 1:13–20. In writing the Colossians, whose faith seems to have been upset by self-styled messengers of the truth who insisted that Christians must perform certain ascetic ceremonies in order to placate the evil powers, Paul declares that the power of the Adversary has already been broken. Christians already share citizenship in the kingdom of God, where through the Son of God forgiveness is not merely a prospect of what might be gained in the end time but a present possession as God's gift.

The one who has made access possible to this new sphere of life is Christ, both image and instrument of God's redemptive purpose in the creation. He makes visible the God whom no man can behold. He is the new model for obedient creatures. He is the agent through which God created the world. Even the powers of the cosmos that are now in rebellion against God, acting as though they were independent of him, were brought into being through him and will ultimately be brought under control by him. Like wisdom in the OT, Christ is both the vehicle through which God's purpose is made known to men and the agency by which it is to be accomplished.

Christ is not to be thought of as a remedy for cosmic difficulties brought in by God after matters had gotten out of control, but as the instrument of his purpose, existing before the world was created and embodying the rationale which makes a sensible whole out of a fragmented and meaningless universe (v. 17). But he is the primary pattern for the church as well: its head, by which it is given direction and coordinated; the archetype by whose life and will it is to be guided; the prototype, on whom rests its hope of victory over death. There is no person or thing that exceeds his significance for the church or that should surpass him in the church's esteem.

There were those in the first century of our era who were worried about passing successfully through the whole range of celestial powers which were thought to stand as obstacles between man and God. Paul declares, rather, that the full range of celestial powers are God's and that all are concretely operative in Jesus. Their function is not one of opposition or hostility but of reconciliation. Through him all the hostile forces within man and throughout the universe will be brought into harmony with the divine purpose. The power of suffering love, as enacted on the cross, is the instrument of this cosmic reconciliation.

Gospel: Luke 23:35–43. Like all those since the time of Jesus who have heard the message of his cross, those who were firsthand observers of his agony and death were divided as to the significance of this gruesome event. Many who had heard his message of the coming of God's kingdom and the certainty of God's vindication of him considered his cruel execution to be a sign that his hopes were vain and his promises were idle boasts. Ironically, they speak the truth when they declare that if he is indeed God's Messiah he cannot save himself. To have accepted escape from the cross would have been to forfeit his messianic role.

Similarly ironic is the inscription "the King of the Jews." The Romans considered him to be an insurrectionist whose aim was to set up a political kingdom, like that of the Maccabees of old. The Jews of his time seem to have been either disillusioned that he did not do so, as was the case with Judas, or they were pleased to have the Romans put him out of the way, even on this trumped-up charge. One of the malefactors, on the other hand, acknowledged his own guilt while affirming Jesus' innocence, and then went on to ask Jesus' intervention in his behalf on the occasion of Jesus' assuming his kingly role. But even in the interim, beginning that very day, Jesus promised that we would be with him in the abode of the blessed dead (v. 43).

Throughout his Gospel, Luke portrays Jesus as concerned for the poor, the outcast, the outsider, the Gentile. In Luke's version of Jesus' sermon at Nazareth (Luke 4), as in the greeting of the infant Jesus by the aged Simeon (Luke 2:29–32), the outreach of the gospel is to men and women in all conditions. Nothing could be more appropriate than to portray a thief, condemned and dying, as the first to acclaim Jesus as God's agent of reconciliation.

HOMILETICAL INTERPRETATION

Today's three readings are easily integrated because of the progression they represent: from Jeremiah's prediction of a righteous king, to Luke's account of the consummation of Jesus' earthly life, to the vision in Colossians of Christ, the firstborn from the dead, as head of the body, the church. It is a picture, in the little, of the saving life, death, and resurrection of Christ which the church lives out each year. This week another such year comes to a close.

Christians often have a poor view of the processes of government. They may not be cynical in this, but realistic. Perhaps they have seen so much demagoguery in politics that they tend to brand the whole business a fraud, the oppression of the common man by those unfit to bear the rule.

An example of this is our tendency to praise Jesus by saying that he was "no mere political messiah." This doubtless means that he was something more and better. Yet the phrase is indicative. "Messiah" is, of course, a technical word for an anointed figure, a king. A messiah therefore cannot be "mere." He is a political leader by definition. If Jesus is a messiah, he is such only figuratively or by accommodation.

Jeremiah is speaking, in the first reading, of shepherds who mislead and scatter God's flock. He is not talking about false religious teachers, despite the tendency of churchmen to appropriate all such imagery to themselves. He has in mind the political and military oligarchy whose policies have brought this once nomadic shepherd people to defeat and exile. His targets are public men whose actions have led to the figurative shearing of the sheep—defeat by the Babylonians and exile to their land.

The hope Jeremiah holds out is not that this people will have pure religious teaching in days to come. No, there will be a political figure raised up, a king who shall govern wisely and reign justly (Jer. 23:5).

What more do people need, really, than to live in peace and security? Free of all fear of tyranny, of being victimized by the rich and the powerful, free of anxiety over family and property, and the loss of sons in foreign wars, they may then have the leisure for prayer. The name of a ruler who will ensure this possibility should fittingly be, says Jeremiah, "the Lord our justice." The prophet's teaching was that a religious people, when threatened by invasion, ought to have as its response a seeking of the wisdom and justice of the Lord in its leadership.

Jeremiah's contempt for Jehoiachin, who ruled during 598 only, was near total. His view of Zedekiah (598–587) was not much better. In place of the latter, whose throne name mean "the Lord is righteous," will come a righteous Branch. The justice of this king will be such that Judah and Israel will be able to give him the name "the Lord is our righteousness" (v. 6). So writes the prophet, in a wordplay on the name of the weak public figure Zedekiah.

It is strange, but in our reading of our Scriptures we tend to assume a stance of superiority toward all matters Jewish. *They* were so earthbound as to want wisdom and justice in government, but *we* have Jesus who will carry us off to heaven when we die. Jesus never taught anything of the sort, of course. He did exhort his hearers to such human decency, such fairness that a canker like the gouging of the poor by the rich could not take hold if they were in the least sensitive to his Father's demands. By theologizing the concept of righteousness almost totally, we have come close to emptying it of its primal meaning of "justice."

A "remnant" for us is a leftover piece of carpeting or yard goods. For our Jewish forebears it was a faithful residue, Jews from "all the countries where I have driven them" who would be brought back to their fold (v. 3). So sure was Isaiah of this promise that he had named one of his sons, a century before Jeremiah's time, *Shear-yashubh,* "a remnant shall return."

It is well to recall this certainty of faith, especially when things are darkest in political life or church life. Jesus never forgot his prophetic legacy. He came to heal the sick, not the well, to call the lost sheep of the house of Israel, to seek and save that which was lost. No dream of mass conversion for him—Clovis's Franks in the river receiving baptism at their ruler's whim; tens of thousands in a stadium confessing Christ; whole nations reckoned "Christian" in demographic yearbooks. Jesus went for the remnant, for the publicans and sinners whom no one else would have, hoping to find in them a remnant of fidelity.

The symbolism is especially fitting because he himself died a felon's death. His companions in death were brigands, *lēstai.* Since he did nothing to save himself, it was assumed that he could not (Luke 23:35).

But one of the criminals gambled on his power, his justice, and made a bid for freedom. He asked for amnesty and he got it.

The criminal who asked Jesus to remember him when he came into his kingly power had a good start on the problem by knowing he was guilty of something. He was being put to death for cause, not for no cause, as was the case with Jesus: "But this man has done nothing wrong" (Luke 23:41). He sought deliverance from the dominion of darkness and transfer to the kingdom of God's beloved Son (cf. Col. 1:13). We have no way of knowing the mentality of this insurrectionist, or even whether he was a common street brawler or a highly motivated Jewish patriot. Did he know his people's history and their longing for a Davidic king of whom it could be said, "The Lord is our righteousness"? Or did he know just enough current history to be sure he wanted the Romans driven off, even at the cost of his life?

Nor can we know how trustworthy a tradition is responsible for the "two thieves" detail or whether their existence depends on the prophecy that a just one was "numbered with the transgressors" (Isa. 53:12). We are left with "redemption and the forgiveness of sins" (Col. 1:14) as God's answer to guilt for an offense. A total denial of human guilt has no place in our Scriptures.

The Colossian hymn finds the fullness of God dwelling in Jesus. Because the Pauline author holds that to be true, much else follows. God's Son is before all; all things were created through him and for him; he is the firstborn of creation; in him all things hold together; he is the head of the body.

This is all splendid christological theory and no believer is disposed to challenge it. But as theory it can remain just that: a gossamer web of cosmic triumph. The question is, does it work? Is there, in fact, any reconciliation achieved? Does Christ make peace by the blood of his cross—which is another way of asking if peace has had any victories since the good thief asked to be remembered? The services of the reconciling Christ are not thrust on anyone. There is the precondition of interest and desire.

The Far Eastern religious traditions make progress in our midst for good reasons and for bad. One of the best reasons is their teaching on the harmony between man and nature. One of the worst is their presentation (as it is thought) of man in a guilt-free condition. This attractiveness represents not so much a virtue of the Asian religions as a double failure in the West: preachers of Judaism and the gospel have not always conveyed the biblical teaching on sin and guilt well; and when they have, the burden has not been acknowledged. The criminal who said, "And we indeed justly; for we are receiving the due reward of our deeds," has not been a popular figure in modern life. We would rather declare paradise an illusion than face the fact of guilt.

Guilt is a good word for a bad reality. It has been turned into a bad word for a neutral reality. The concept has been so thoroughly misconceived that the term more usually stands for false guilt or guilt feelings that correspond to no wrongdoing, than for the real thing. There is lots of real guilt around, or should be if we had not rationalized the notion away. Simple greed, unenlightened self-interest, unconcern for the fate of the other. There are any number of ways to describe the dominion of darkness.

Gautama was described by the followers as the Enlightened One. This sleeper came awake by virtue of his awareness, his *bodhi*, his wisdom. Jesus' followers made a similar claim for their Teacher. They called their own Buddha nature "the inheritance of the saints in light." Christ was the image of God, this man whom they viewed as the center of creation. Himself the just one, he was the dispenser of justice, the reconciler of warring factions among brothers and within the individual. He offered peace—an ancient Persian term is *paradise*—if the resistor would but stop resisting, the struggler give up his struggle.

No self-laceration is required for the reconciliation that brings peace, only a facing of reality.

Self-delusion brings no peace: "How can there be forgiveness? I am guilty of nothing."

"Do you not fear God, since you are under the same sentence of condemnation?"

Being sons or daughters of Adam has put us under that sentence, not in any mythical sense but in stark reality. To be human, simply to be, is to be prone to self-seeking and darkness. There is a kingdom of light which is not inherently in ourselves. It is in another, in Christ who is all light.

We must acknowledge guilt. We must admit the light.